Hi

CW00402446

Stanislav Samuhel

Mountain Walks in the High Tatra

Translated by Andrea Adelung

50 selected walks in the High Tatra

With 56 colour photographs
and 50 colour Freytag & Berndt walking maps on a scale of 1:50,000
and 1:75,000

ROTHER · MUNICH

Front cover photo:
Popradské pleso lake, in the background Kôprovský štít (centre) and
Volovec (right).

Frontispiece (photo on page 2):
A meadow in Dolina Bieleho potoka valley, behind it, Kolový štít.

All photographs taken by the author, with the exception of the photos on
pages 26, 55 (M. Legutky) and 106 (J. Bobula).

Walking maps on a scale of 1:50,000 and 1:75,000
© Freytag & Berndt, Vienna

Translation: C. Ade Team (Andrea Adelung)

3rd edition 2001
© Bergverlag Rother GmbH, Munich
ISBN 3-7633-4810-7

Distributed in Great Britain by Cordee, 3a De Montfort Street, Leicester
Great Britain LE1 7HD, www.cordee.co.uk
in USA by AlpenBooks, 3616 South Road, C-1, Mukilteo,
WA 98275 USA, www.alpenbooks.com

Preface

The High Tatra represents the only mountain range in Slovakia possessing an alpine character – even though it is one of the smallest mountain ranges in Europe. The strongly structured forms of its peaks were formed by glaciers, which shaped them millennia ago. Due to a climatic warming, the valley glaciers gradually melted completely. Thus, the natural barrier disappeared which had protected the mountains from the influences of civilizations for ages.

This made the High Tatra easily accessible. People began to penetrate the mountain range, and in the last 200 years, the High Tatra was made accessible to such a degree that, today, it represents a popular holiday area.

Comfortable walking paths lead through the valleys, crossings adorn several saddles, and twenty summits are accessible via marked paths. Tourists seeking relaxation also have several options to become familiar with the Tatra. The highest spa town in the High Tatra, Štrbské Pleso, 1355 m, is accessible via car and mountain railway; the panoramic elevation Hrebienok, 1285 m, can be reached via a ground cableway, the mountain valley Skalnatá dolina, 1751 m, via two cableways, and a further cableway runs up to the second-highest summit in the High Tatra, the Lomnický štít, 2632 m. On the mountain lake Velické pleso, a mountain hotel is located at an elevation of 1670 m, and at the foot of the saddle sedlo Váha, 2250 m, a hut can be found. On the slopes of Solisko, 1830 m, and under the saddle Lomnické sedlo, 2125 m, one can catch a chair lift to the top. From there, the ridges of the High Tatra, which reach elevations of over 2500 m at certain points, are easily accessible, such that even less experienced tourists are able to enjoy picturesque ascents without long marches.

With the development of tourism, especially after 1945, the number of visitors to the High Tatra increased dramatically, which also brought with it two undesirable phenomena: damage to nature and several accidents in the mountains. In order to put an end to these problems, the Tatra National Park was put to law in 1949, and in 1950, the Mountain Service was established. Among its tasks are environmental protection and conservation of the natural splendour in this area, obligation to precision with regard to the network of paths, the safety of the visitors in the mountains and mountain rescue and mountain guide services. The High Tatra is easy to reach, but this should not lead to people overestimating their capabilities. Only those who undertake hikes corresponding to their abilities will reach the true goal of a stay in the High Tatra: getting to know the beauty of the mountains while at the same time being able to relax and have a perfect time.

Tatranská Lomnica, Spring 2001   Stanislav and Ľubomír Samuhel

Contents

Tourist Information

Using This Guide

The Table of Contents shows the destinations of the individual mountain walks, which are organized according to starting points, progressing from west to east. For each route suggestion, the most important information is first listed in abbreviated form, followed by a detailed description of the route. The course of the routes is displayed in accompanying maps. A colour photograph reflects the character of the route destination and its environs. An important component of the guide is the index at the end of the book. It lists all route destinations, starting points, shelters and huts, the most important summits, saddles, valleys and lakes. This facilitates the hiker's orientation.

A few of the walks can also be undertaken in the opposite direction, or can be combined with another corresponding route. The directions described in this guide, however, are usually more advantageous, and any continuation of the hike depends on the condition of its participants.

In Mengusovská dolina valley. Satan in the background.

Grade

Most of the walks follow well-maintained and marked walkways and paths. However, this should not blur the fact that sure-footedness and a lack of vertigo are still necessary in some parts. In addition, note that the tours can exhibit increased difficulties in early summer and after longer periods of inclement weather. In order to be able to better assess the demands of individual tours, the numbers of all route suggestions are colour-coded. These colours are to be interpreted as follows:

BLUE

The path is well marked and, for the most part, only moderately steep. These walks can also be undertaken by children and elderly persons under normal conditions (fair weather, no snow cover). They require no special equipment or physical condition.

RED

These routes are well marked, but often narrow and steep. They should only be undertaken by mountain hikers who are sure-footed and properly equipped.

BLACK

Most of these hikes are also adequately marked, but are narrow and include long stretches of steep sections. They may be very exposed in places and sometimes require the use of the hands. This means that these walks should only be done by experienced mountain hikers who are absolutely sure-footed, in strong physical condition, and are experienced in alpine hiking. Only permitted in the company of a mountain guide!

You will see this piece of information under »Grade« for many of the »black« and unmarked hikes which, in accordance with National Park regulations, may only be undertaken with a mountain guide. Violation of this regulation may result in a fine! Note: Some sections of these tours may require a safety rope!

Equipment

Sturdy walking shoes with a good tread, clothing appropriate for the weather conditions, a rucksack with a pullover, hat, anorak, waterproofs and/or sun protection, provisions and enough to drink (no alcohol), as well as a first-aid kit are recommended. Only in the case of leisurely walks (»blue« routes) will simple leisure clothing suffice.

Dangers

Sudden changes in the weather, accompanied by the passing of a cold front, can turn the hiking paths at altitudes of over 1600 m into snowy terrain, even in the middle of summer. Therefore, it is essential to turn back from the higher elevations in a timely manner at the first signs of inclement weather. Furthermore, firn fields can linger into early summer in some leeward inclines, mainly on northern and eastern slopes, which make mountain tours impossible to continue. You can find out about snow conditions and accessibility of the paths from the Mountain Service of the TANAP, either in person or by telephone in Starý Smokovec.

Maps
Each tour suggestion is accompanied by an illustrated map of the route. This map excerpt is enough to complete the walk. To obtain a better overview of the entire mountain range as well as any connection possibilities with other routes, the summer tourist map of the High Tatra is recommended, which indicates the marked paths with colours corresponding to the markers along the path (red, blue, green, yellow, black). When estimating the length of time a tour will take, keep in mind that it is not the distance but primarily the degree of incline and difficulty, especially in rocky terrain, which are decisive. That is why the signs in the National Park indicate duration in hours instead of distance in km. The summer tourist map can only be used during periods without snow cover.

Walking Times
The walking times indicated correspond to the pace of an average tourist. They only reflect the actual walking time, not including breaks and rest time. The entire duration is indicated, as well as the times for the individual sections.

Huts and Cableways
Due to the short valley lengths in the High Tatra, it is not absolutely necessary to stay overnight in the shelter huts maintained in the summer season. However, those wishing to spend several days in a hut must make a reservation in advance through a travel agent. Almost every hut has a telephone. The huts are closed in the off-season, from autumn to Christmas and sometimes also in the spring. The same applies for the cableways.

The National Border
Almost one-fifth of the High Tatra is situated in Poland. The national border runs from the west on the main ridge to the Rysy summit, and continues along the secondary ridge northward into the Bielovodská dolina valley. Six of the described routes converge on this border, namely: Hladský štít (Tour 2), Mengusovské sedlo (Tour 10), Rysy (Tour 11) Bielovodská dolina (Tour 42), Hrubý štít (Tour 45) and Svinica (Tour 50). Crossing the national borders in the hiking terrain is not permitted! You may only cross the border where a

A typical valley of the High Tatra with a divided crest at the end of the valley.

customs and passport control point are located. In the High Tatra, this is only possible at the Lysá poľana border crossing. If, as a result of bad weather, an accident or having gotten lost, you should nevertheless wind up in foreign territory, you are obligated to register with the border authorities in that country.

Tips for Mountain Hikers

- Only select walks which correspond to your capabilities.
- Find out in advance about the current conditions on the paths.
- Before embarking on a long tour, inform your place of accommodation about the destination of your walk, and provide the estimated time of your return.
- Begin the tour in the morning and never walk alone. Having the appropriate equipment and paying attention to weather developments will guarantee your safety.
- In case you are travelling without a guide, do not leave the marked walkways.
- Do not walk on snowfields in the summer. If a walkway is covered with snow in terrain above the tree line, and there are no pole markers, the path is considered to be unmarked, and you should break off the walk.

Rules for Visitors to the Tatra National Park

The entire area of the High Tatra, including the Belianske Tatry, Belaen Tatra and Západné Tatry ranges, as well as the Western Tatra, have all been declared part of the Tatra National Park.

This obligates visitors to adhere to regulations during walks and stays in the area, which serve to conserve nature and protect its natural beauty. These regulations are contained in the »Visitor Regulations of the TANAP« as well as the directory of tourist pathways that are seasonally closed. The main point of the Visitor Regulations is a limitation of the hikes allowed to the official, marked trails. This, of course, does not include public roads, communities, and their immediate surroundings. This limitation is also valid in the Polish National Park.

The trails and pathways are marked with a symbol consisting of three horizontal stripes, whereby the middle stripe is coloured, and the outer two are white. Off of the marked trails and pathways, tourists are only permitted to hike in the company of a mountain guide, with the exception of mountain climbers who are undertaking climbing tours and are in possession of a valid identity card from their national Alpine club (SAC, DAV, ÖAV, CAF, CAI and others).

In the winter and spring, usually during the period from 1 November to 30 June, some marked trails and pathways are closed. If you wish to take a tour outside of the summer season, we recommend inquiring at the Mountain Service Office in Starý Smokovec, tel.: 2820. The Visitor Regulations as well as a complete index of all closed trails are available in the museum of the TANAP in Tatranská Lomnica or in the Mountain Service Office in Starý Smokovec, where you can also hire a mountain guide. Other, special regulations apply to mountain climbers. To find out about the regulations valid for the Polish National Park TPN, you can inquire at the information stand of the TPN Zakopane at the »Rondo« intersection.

Useful Information

Mountains and Valleys

The High Tatra, the highest mountain range of the 1200-km long Carpathian Arch, is situated in northern Slovakia, and its rocky ridges set the range off markedly from bordering mountain chains, with their grassy mountain ridges. To the west, from the saddle Ľaliové sedlo, it is designated as the Western Tatra, »Západné Tatry«, with the highest peak being Bystrá, 2248 m; to the east, from the saddle Kopské sedlo, known as the Belaen Tatra, »Belianske Tatry«, with Havran, 2152 m. The main crest of the High Tatra has a length of 26 km, and, together with the tributary crests, forms over 30 valleys. Four valleys on the northwestern side are situated in Polish territory. The High Tatra possesses five large peaks. These are, from west to east: Kriváň, 2494 m; then the jewel of the range, Vysoká, 2560 m; the highest peak, Gerlachovský štít, 2655 m, in the middle of this mountain chain; in the northeast, the mighty Ľadový, 2627 m, and in the east, the peak of Lomnický štít, 2632 m. The majority of the mountain peaks has sharp, craggy, rocky ridges, and plunge into the valleys with steep rock walls. On some of these precipitous peaks, however, there is an accessible ascent route on at least one side, which even enables hikers to reach the summit. These summits are popular for that reason, and tours to them are also included in this guide.

The main crest is shaped like a semi-arch stretching from the northwest to the southeast, and curving in the middle to the south. The axis of most of the valleys runs perpendicular to this direction. The valleys were once formed by glaciers; they have wide valley floors, and from the mouth to the end of the valley, they do not ascend gradually, but rather in a step-like fashion, with the formation of terraces that are separated from one another by steep swells. On the terraces, two types of lakes can be observed: cirque lakes, which are usually located in the higher rock basins that have been hollowed out by glaciers, and moraine lakes on natural embankments which have been formed by piles of rock stemming from glaciers mainly in the mouths of valleys. On the Slovakian side, the two largest lakes are Veľké Hincovo pleso and Štrbské pleso, both with an area of 20 hectares, while in the Polish part of the High Tatra, there are even larger lakes. The largest, Morski Oko, has an area of 35 hectares, and the deepest, Wielki Staw, has a depth of 79 m. There are over 100 lakes, many of them in the valley of Veľká Studená dolina.

The lakes are the jewels of the High Tatra; with their water, they give life to the individual valleys. Many are steeped in legend. They have various colours – some of the lakes are even named after these colours. These lakes are among the most frequented tourist destinations. Waterfalls have developed on some of the steps between terraces over which streams run. The most well known of them include the 25-cm high waterfall Skok, and the waterfalls of the mountain stream Studený potok. Among the highest waterfalls are Kmeťov vodopád and Český vodopád, as well as the 70-m high Siklawa in Polish territory.

The Plant World
In the lowest elevations of the foothills, under 800 m, there is a sub-mountainous step with land used for agriculture. The step of the coniferous forests extends from the lower tree line, which more or less also makes up the border of the Tatra National Park: mostly spruce woods, on the southwest slopes of the High Tatra mixed with mountain pines, in the eastern part, with fir trees, and in higher elevations, with Swiss stone pines, which decorate these woods. The Swiss stone pines have a crown-like shape in the valleys and reach a few hundred years of age. Solitary trees growing high on precipices and exposed to the wind have a flag-like shape. Where there is limestone earth, beech and maples trees can be found, especially between the High and the Belaen Tatra. The upper tree line runs along the south side of the mountain range at an elevation of 1550 m, on the north side at about 1400 m. The sub-alpine step stretches out above the forest, where mountain pines primarily grow. There, high-mountain meadows can also be found, with a rich array of plants. Above 2300 m, the terrain is rocky, and plants are rare. On the

The snowy peaks of the High Tatra after a summer period of cold air.

The eastern part of the High Tatra with the peaks Kolový, Kozí and Jahňací štít.

summit of Gerlachovský štít and its environs, botanists have nevertheless found approximately 20 types of plants.

The Animal World

In the High Tatra all animals apart from foxes are protected by law. In the forests, there is a predominance of red deer; roe deer, on the other hand, are less prevalent. There are also a few lynx. Wild boars often live in the foothills. In the last decades, bears have increased in number, and these herbivores can sometimes be found on hiking paths. Above the forests, we find the realm of the chamois and the groundhog. These types of animals have suffered in the past due to an excess of tourist and ski traffic in the valleys. When their numbers dwindled significantly, the Tatra National Park administration closed a few valleys and portions of areas from 1 November to 30 June. According to the counts taken by the foresters, almost 600 chamois and 800 groundhogs live in the area of the High Tatra. About 6 pairs of eagles have eyries in the inaccessible rock walls. Weasels and ermines can be found on mountain summits, especially those often visited by tourists. Ravens circle above the mountain crests, and shy fir jays make their homes in the vicinity of the Swiss stone pines.

Locations and Starting points

Tatranská Javorina, 1000 m

A small mountain community at the foot of the northern crest of the Belianske Tatry and Vysoké Tatry mountains. It was built up around the former iron foundry, which was established in the mid-18th century. There is a guesthouse and a forester's house in the community. Not far from the town, approximately 1 km away, is the Hotel Poľana and a hunting lodge, which was once the seat of Prince Hohenlohe. The castle was built at the end of the 19th century. On the western edge of town, there is a ski field with a ski lift, and beneath it, a wooden church.

Tatranská Javorina is the starting point of tours into the valleys of Javorová dolina and Zadné Meďodoly. There are bus connections. It is 27 km to Tatranská Lomnica, and to the border town of Lysá poľana (national border between Slovakia and Poland) 3 km.

Lysá poľana, 970 m

Small settlement on the Slovakian/Polish border in the mouth of the valley Bielovodská dolina. The small river Biela voda, which forms the border, divides the community in a Polish and a Slovakian part. In the Slovakian part, there is a guesthouse, a building of the Tatra National Park and the old customs office. In the Polish part, there is the new customs office and a petrol station.

Bus connections. Distance to Tatranská Lomnica 30 km, to Zakopane 20 km.

Podbanské, 940 m

A tourist community, bus stop, hotel. The nearest campground is located in Vavrišovo, 13 km to the southwest. To Štrbské Pleso, 17 km.

Starý Smokovec, 1010 m

The most significant town in the High Tatra, the seat of the Administration, was founded at the end of the 18th century. The town developed from its original form as a climatic health resort into a tourism centre. It is the starting point of mountain tours in the central portion of the mountain chain. There are five hotels here, several holiday homes, a rental office for sporting equipment, an ice-skating rink, the mountain service, the service centre for mountain guides, an information centre of the TANAP, a travel agency, a doctor's office, a pharmacy, an automotive service and a department store; in addition, there is a beautiful wooden church and two painting galleries.

The nearest campground is located 3 km away in the direction of Poprad. There is a ground cableway to the panoramic hill of Hrebienok. Travel connections with the mountain railway and bus. To Štrbské Pleso 16 km, to Tatranská Lomnica 6 km, to Poprad (railway station, airfield) 12 km.

Štrbské Pleso, 1355 m
A climatic health resort situated on the slopes of the moraine wall of the lake of the same name beneath the mouth of the valley Mlynická dolina. In the year 1872, the first hut was erected in this town. The health resort was founded in 1881; the latest modern buildings date from the time of the ski world championships, which took place here in 1970. Currently, there are four hotels here, a few restaurants, a department store, the end station of the mountain railway from Poprad and Tatranská Lomnica, as well as the cog railway from Tatranská Štrba, a ski centre with ski jumping hill and cross-country trails. The nearest campground is located in Tatranská Štrba (8 km). Bus connections. To Starý Smokovec 16 km, to Podbanské 17 km.

Tatranská Lomnica, 850 m
A spa town that was founded in 1892. It is situated at the foot of the mountain Lomnický štít. Protected from the surrounding woods, Tatranská Lomnica possesses the mildest climate of all of the towns in the High Tatra. It houses

The village of Mengusovce with the peaks of Gerlachovský štít and Bradavica.

the seat of the Tatra National Park Administration. A Nature Conservation Museum with exhibits on nature, history and folklore of the region exists here, as do five hotels, two tourist accommodations, and several holiday homes. A ski centre with two ski lifts, ski jumping hills, and cross-country trails are located on the western edge of town. On the northwestern edge, there is a small, neo-Gothic church and a miniature golf course, and on the north-eastern edge there is a botanical garden. To the southeast of town, in the direction of Veľká Lomnica, there are three campgrounds that also have an automotive service. There are railway and bus connections in several directions, and a mountain railway. To Starý Smokovec 6 km, to the climatic health resort Štrbské Pleso 21 km, to Lysá poľana and the national border to Poland 30 km. To the mountain lake Skalnaté pleso 2 cableways.

Tatranská Polianka, 1000 m
A climatic health resort in the middle of fir woods at the mouth of the valley Velická dolina. It was founded at the end of the 19th century, and was known as a busy sports town until 1945. Currently, the local spa establishments serve solely for the curing of respiratory illnesses. A restaurant is present, however without overnight accommodation. Mountain railway, bus connection. To Starý Smokovec 4 km, to the spa town Štrbské Pleso 12 km.

Vyšné Hágy, 1100 m
Spa town that is divided into two parts by the mountain railway. The spa facilities are located in the upper part, and the small settlement in the lower part. The lower part of the settlement came into being when Count Mariássy had the first small tourist hotel built (1891). The spa facilities were built by the state in the year 1940. At that time, it was the largest spa facility for healing respiratory illnesses in Central Europe. No accommodations for tourists. Bus connections. To Starý Smokovec 9 km, to Štrbské Pleso 7 km.

Zakopane
An extensive summer holiday resort beneath the northern slopes of the High and West Tatra, built up on hilly meadows between 800 and 1000 m sea level. With 30 000 inhabitants and over two million visitors each year, Zakopane is the largest tourist centre of the entire mountain range. Founded at the end of the 13th century, it only became a summer holiday resort after the arrival of Pastor J. Stolarczyk, who, in 1850, built the first church, a school, and a presbytery in the formerly backward mountain village, which quickly progressed, and by the end of the 19th century, had grown into a »summer holiday resort« and a spa town. Currently, visitors can choose from ten hotels, countless private rooms for let, two campgrounds, two tent campsites, a department store, four travel agencies, an automotive service – and a hospital. The seat of the administration of the Polish National park TPN and the

Morskie Oko lake and Rysy, from Kępa mountain.

central office of the mountain rescue service with a heliport are located here. Among the things worth seeing are, above all, five museums; the largest of them, the »Chalubinski Museum«, is located in the centre of town. Several wooden buildings are noteworthy, especially the old church dating from 1850, the church of Apostle St. John from the 18th century, the villa »dom pod Jedlami« from 1897 on Koziniec, the villa »Witkiewiczówna« from 1904 on Antalówka, and several others. In the upper part of town, there is a ski centre with two ski jumping hills, built in the year 1962 for the ski world championship FIS. Further south, a four-kilometre long cableway leads from Kuźnice up to the main crest, to the mountain Kasprowy Wierch. In the lower part of town, the valley station of the ground cableway to Gubałówka can be found, from where you can get the best view of the town and its surroundings, including the entire chain of Tatra peaks, of which the nearest, Giewont, 1984 m, dominates, with an easily visible summit cross.

Zakopane is so rich in various sights, that two days are not enough for a visit to this town. There are bus connections to the border town of Lysá poľana (national border between Poland and Slovakia), 23 km, to Tatranská Lomnica another 31 km.

Ždiar, 895 m

A town situated between the mountains of Spišska Magura and Belianske Tatry. Not too long ago, this was still a typical mountain village with several small settlements on the nearby hills; however, in the last two decades, it has lost its original character. Every independent economic settlement consisted of a three-room residence, which, together with the farm buildings, formed a square outline with an enclosed courtyard, which was protected from snowstorms and wild animals. The folk dress has disappeared from daily life; sometimes one can still see it on Sundays in front of the church or at performances of the local folklore ensemble Ždiaranček. A Ždiar room preserved as a museum with original furnishings, as well as an original Ždiar household, give the visitor an impression of the former way of life. There is a restaurant here and private accommodation opportunities. Bus connections. To Tatranská Lomnica 15 km.

Excursion Destinations and Sites of Natural Beauty

Belianska jaskyňa
Limestone cave in the northern slope of the mountain Kobylí vrch, which is located above the spa town Tatranská Kotlina, 7 km away from Ždiar. The entrance to the cave is located at an elevation of 885 m, the length of the passages amounts to 4 km (1 km open to the public). Stalactite/stalagmite formations in the cave, a few large halls and small lakes. They were discovered by treasure hunters in the 18th century and opened to the public in the year 1882. Since 1896, the cave has had electrical lighting, the first in Europe.

Dolina Bieleho potoka
A small valley covered with meadows southwest of the community of Tatranská Javorina, beneath the forests of the mountain Gombošov vrch. From here, there is a breathtaking view of Jahňací štít and Kolový štít, and to the right, of Široká. At the beginning of this small valley, there is a wooden church and a cemetery with the grave of Prince Hohenlohe, who once owned Tatranská Javorina and the surrounding valleys.

Tichá dolina
At 14 km, the longest valley of the High Tatra. Due to its location off the beaten track of tourist centres, it is not frequently visited. Thus, it primarily offers a pleasant time to those who are looking for tranquil natural scenery. The mountain peaks of Svinica and Kapsrov vrch at the end of the valley are highly frequented, but almost exclusively from the north (from the Polish side).

Kobylia dolina
A grass-covered sloping valley with a magical vista into the valley Temné smreciny, its two lakes and the waterfall Vajanského vodopád. In the lower part of the valley of Kobylia dolina, east of the hiking trail, lies the small lake Kobylie pleso, 1734 m, which is gradually disappearing.

Litorové pleso, 1863 m
An unexpectedly beautiful lake with a rich array of plants situated in a desolate valley basin. It has an area of 1.7 hectares, a depth of 19 m and a length of 170 m. A fantastic view of the faces of the opposing Kačací. Good resting spot. Its name stems from the medicinal plant litvor (arch angelica), which is common in the environs of the lake (see Tour 42).

Skalnaté pleso, 1751 m
The name of the mountain lake and the small settlement in its vicinity. Mountain station of the cableway from Tatranská Lomnica. Observatory, the buildings of the two cableways are connected, two huts. Mountain service

station, valley station of the chair lift to the Lomnické sedlo crest. The lake has an inconsistent amount of water, and sometimes dries out, which is a consequence of damage to the moraine wall during the construction of the cableway. An unmarked walking path circles the lake. The surrounding mountains: from the left, the mountain crest Lomnický hrebeň, 2211 m, the saddle Lomnické sedlo, 2190 m, the peak Lomnický štít, 2632 m, the ridge Vidlové veže, and beneath it, three basins of the so-called Cmiter, as well as the peak Kežmarský štít, 2558 m, and Huncovský štít, 2351 m.

Slavkovská vyhliadka, 1521 m
An enhanced panoramic hill. It dates from the year 1905, and was subsequently also named »Maximilian Hill« in honour of Dr. Maximilian Weisz, who had the hill built, along with the pathway. From there, one has an astounding view of the depths of both valleys Veľká a Malá and Studená dolina, as well as the western face of the mountain peak Lomnický štít.

Symbolic Cemetery, 1525 m
The cemetery with a small chapel is located near the lake Popradské pleso. Here, there are commemorative plaques to the tourists and mountain climbers who lost their lives in the High Tatra. It was erected in the year 1940. The plaques on granite blocks, with their carved ornaments, complement the decorative wooden crosses made by the folk artist J. Fekiač from Detva. The number of all victims of fatal accidents in the High Tatras that have been recorded over history since 1771 amounts to almost 880. However, there are only about 200 plaques.
A few of the plaques are worth noting, due to their remarkable artistic design or historical importance. Among others, you can find the plaques of two famous mountain guides, Johann Franz from the town of Nová Lesná, and Klimek Bachleda from Zakopane, as well as the plaques of the legendary Polish mountain climber W. Stanisklawski, and a plaque dedicated to the seven members of the mountain rescue service who in 1979 perished during rescue efforts related to a helicopter crash.

Huncovská vyhliadka, 1877 m
Vista point at the fork of the tourist pathway above the observatory at the mountain station of the cableway from Tatranská Lomnica to Skalnaté pleso. A rest area with a beautiful view of the Levočské vrchy mountains.

Lomnická vyhliadka, 1529 m
Vista point with a covered bench on the rocky edge of the Lomnický hrebeň crest. A view of the valleys Veľká a Malá and Studená dolina, of the mountain slopes of Slavkovský štít and the Zips foothills of the High Tatra from the town of Kežmarok in the east, to the town of Svit in the south.

A Small Glossary of the Most Important Expressions

Slovakian	English	Polish
vrch	mountain	wierzch
štít	peak	szczyt
vrchol	summit, peak	wierzchołek
veža	tower	turnia
skalná ihla	rock needle	igła skalna
výšvih	uplift	uskok
hrebeň	ridge, crest	grań, grzebień
svah	slope	stok
stena	wall, face	ściana
zráz	precipice	pochyłość
sedlo	saddle	siodło, przełęcz
štrbina	wind gap	szczerbina
žľab (malý)	gully	rynna
žľab	gorge	żleb
kotol (kotlina)	basin (valley basin)	kocioł
dolina	valley	dolina
pleso	lake	staw
potok	stream	potok
vodopád	waterfall	wodospad
cesta	path, way	droga
chodník	path(way), trail	ścieżka, perć
stopy chodníka	path traces	ślady perci
priechod	passageway	przejście
značený chodník	marked path(way)	szlak znakowany
rázcestie	fork	rozstaj dróg, rozdroże
rázcestník	sign(post)	drogowskaz
chata	hut	schronisko
horská železnica	mountain railway	kolejka elektryczna
lanovka	cableway	kolejka linowa
pozemná lanovka	ground cableway	kolejka linowo-szynowa
sedačkový vyťah	chairlift	wyciąg krzesełkowy
vlek	ski lift	wyciąg narciarski
horná stanica	top station	górna stacja
dolná stanica	valley station	dolna stacja
zastávka	(station) stop	przystanek
stupeň ťažkosti	difficulty grade	stopień trudności
istenie na lane	safety rope	asekuracja na linie
pád kameňov	falling rock	spadek kamieniów
snehové pole	firn field	pole śniegu
reťaze	chains	łańcuchy
kramle	cramps	klamry
Horská služba	mountain service	Pogotowie górskie
horský vodca	mountain guide	przewodnik górski

1 Kriváň, 2494 m

To the highest peak of the western section of the High Tatras

Tri Studničky – Priehyba – Kriváň – Jamské pleso

Location: Podbanské, 940 m.
Starting point: The Važecká chata shelter hut, 1180 m. From Podbanské, 5 km by car or bus. 11 km from the climatic health resort Štrbské Pleso.
Parking: Car park at the bus stop close to the Važecká chata hut.
Walking Times: Kriváň 3 hrs.; descent via Priehyba 2½ hrs.; past Jamské pleso lake 3 hrs., total walking time 6 hrs.

Grade: There is a rubble-covered slope in the gorge below the summit; the last section on the summit leads through rocks (path). The entire tour is marked.
Highest point: Kriváň, 2494 m.
Refreshments/Accommodation: The Važecká chata hut (Chata kpt. Rašu), no overnight accommodation available.
Sights: The view from the summit of the High, Low and West Tatras.

The Kriváň is a prominent peak – the first which can be seen when looking from the southwest toward the High Tatra. The rocky faces of the peak plunge steeply downward on all sides; only on the southwestern side does the Kriváň slope gently. Our ascent leads along the left edge of that slope, while the

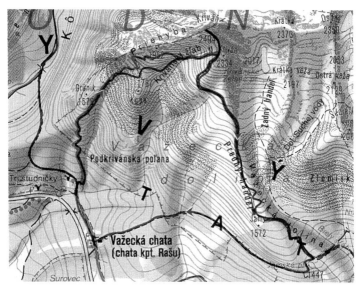

Kriváň from Podbanské.

descent follows along the right side. The Kriváň was known as early as the 15th century, when mining was begun on its slopes. The galleries, some of them caved in, in which gold was derived from the ore mined there, can also be seen today, not far from our ascent. It has been ascertained that miners climbed to the summit in those days as well.

Starting in front of the **Važecká chata** hut (Chata kpt. Rašu) on the forest trail, head northwest (red and green markers) to the signpost at the old forester's house. From here, continue on the green-markered walkway up through the forest, and after ten minutes, through the partially wooded Podkrivánska poľana mountain meadow, and on the southern slopes up to the **Priehyba** saddle (1990 m); 1½ hrs. Here, the walkway departs from the previous direction and heads more towards the right into the gorge, to the signpost, 2120 m. From the south, a blue-markered walkway appears, along which we continue our tour up to the **Daxnerovo sedlo** saddle. From here, there is a terrific view of the ridges of the High Tatras. Deep in the Važecká dolina valley, you can see Krivánske Zelené pleso lake, 2017 m, to the right the elevation of the southern ridge, 2334 m, called Malý Kriváň. From the saddle, head to the left along the cliffs of the southern ridge to the **summit**; ¾ hr.

The **descent** leads along the ascent path up to the signpost in the gorge. From here, follow the blue-markered path to **Jamské pleso** lake (an ideal resting place), and along the red-markered path to the south and west, to the **Važecká chata** hut. From the lake, you can follow the red-markered path to the northeast, to the climatic health resort **Štrbské Pleso**, 1 hour.

2   Závory, 1879 m, and Hladký štít, 2066 m

A rocky peak over elongated, grassy valleys

Podbanské – Kôprová dolina – sedlo Závory – Hladký štít

Location: Podbanské, 940 m.
Starting point: Signpost near the parking area in the middle of town.
Walking Times: Podbanské – signpost under the Grúnik slope, 1¼ hrs., through Kôprová dolina valley to the fork below Temné smrečiny valley, 1½ hrs., to the Závory saddle, 1¼ hrs., to the Hladký sedlo, ¼ hr., to the Hladký štít summit ¼ hr. Ascent 4½ hrs. in total, descent via Tichá dolina valley, 5 hrs., through Kôprová dolina 4 hrs. Total walking time 9 to 10 hrs.

Grade: Through the Kôprová dolina a comfortable road, in higher elevations a maintained path which is marked up to the Hladké sedlo saddle. Rocky terrain to the summit, occasionally only traces of the path.
Highest point: Hladký štít, 2066 m.
Refreshments/Accommodation: Four shelters in Kôprová dolina valley only offer shelter from rain.

The Závory saddle separates the grass-covered tributary crest Liptovské kopy from the primary crest of the High Tatra. The Liptovské kopy massif is a strictly-preserved part of the National Park; entering this area, even with a mountain guide, is prohibited.

From the signpost in **Podbanské** on the street (yellow markers), walk over the bridge and 200 m to the next signpost. Here, head left onto the access

Beneath Závory saddle on the path into Temné smrečiny valley

road to reach the **Tichá** forest house in ½ hour. Head to the right through the **Kôprová dolina** valley (green markers) to the fork beneath the Grúnik slope, 1104 m. You can also access this spot from the Važecká chata hut. Continue on a comfortable path along the Kôprovský potok stream. Higher, along a more steep path, we reach the fork beneath the Hlinská dolina valley, 1411 m (1¼ hours), and, in about ¼ hour, continue along the green waymarked path to the fork beneath Temné smrečiny valley. If you do not

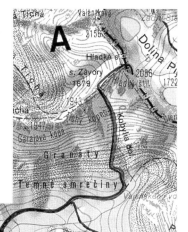

wish to climb to the summit, you can climb to the shores of **Nižné Temnosmrečinské pleso** lake, situated in a romantic basin at the foot of the rocky faces of the Čubrina and Kôprovský štít 1674 m, along a red-markered path in about 1 hour. Our route leads to the left at the fork over the steep swell of Kobylia dolina valley through meadows, and to the **Závory** saddle, where the green waymarks end. From the saddle, we travel straight across the northwestern slope of the **Hladký štít**, on a red-markered walkway to the **Hladké sedlo** saddle. Continuing to the right, onto a rocky mountain ridge, which is not always marked, we head on to the **summit**.

The **descent** follows along the same route to the Závory saddle.

3 Vyšné Kôprovské sedlo, 2180 m

Through three valleys of the tributary ridge Rázsocha Kriváňa

Tri studnicky – Kôprová dolina – Vyšné Kôprovské sedlo – Popradské

Location: Štrbské Pleso, 1355 m.
Starting point: The Važecká chata hut (Chata kpt. Rašu), 1180 m. No overnight Accommodation. From Štrbské Pleso 11 km, from Podbanské 5.5 km. Bus connections.
Parking: The car park is located at the bus stop near the Važecká chata hut. For the return trip, the car park in the town of Štrbské Pleso is more convenient.
Walking Times: Važecká chata hut – fork beneath the Grúnik hill, 1 hr., through the Kôprová dolina valley 1 ¼ hr., through the

Hlinská dolina to the Vyšné Kôprovské sedlo saddle 2¼ hrs., descent to Lake Popradské pleso 1¼ hrs., further into the town of Štrbské Pleso 1¼ hr., total walking time 7 hrs.
Grade: Mountain and forest paths. Only the descent from the saddle is a bit steeper. The route is marked.
Highest point: Vyšné Kôprovské sedlo, 2180 m.
Refreshments/Accommodation: Four open shelters in the Kôprová dolina valley and the house shelter chata Popradské pleso.

The Vyšné Kôprovské sedlo passageway opens up an unexpectedly beautiful view of the mountain peaks surrounding the Mengusovská dolina valley, of

Vyšné Kôprovské sedlo and the Vysoká peak from Hlinská dolina valley.

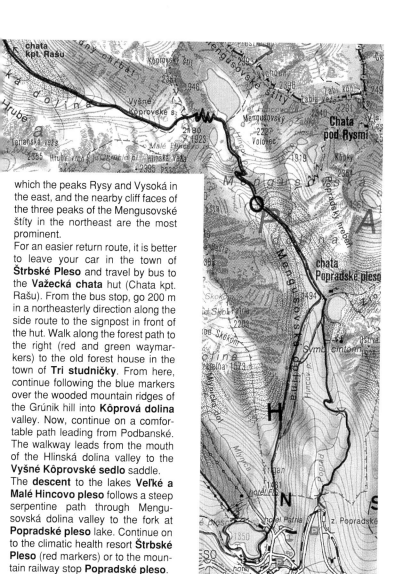

which the peaks Rysy and Vysoká in the east, and the nearby cliff faces of the three peaks of the Mengusovské štíty in the northeast are the most prominent.

For an easier return route, it is better to leave your car in the town of **Štrbské Pleso** and travel by bus to the **Važecká chata** hut (Chata kpt. Rašu). From the bus stop, go 200 m in a northeasterly direction along the side route to the signpost in front of the hut. Walk along the forest path to the right (red and green waymarkers) to the old forest house in the town of **Tri studničky**. From here, continue following the blue markers over the wooded mountain ridges of the Grúnik hill into **Kôprová dolina** valley. Now, continue on a comfortable path leading from Podbanské. The walkway leads from the mouth of the Hlinská dolina valley to the **Vyšné Kôprovské sedlo** saddle.

The **descent** to the lakes **Veľké a Malé Hincovo pleso** follows a steep serpentine path through Mengusovská dolina valley to the fork at **Popradské pleso** lake. Continue on to the climatic health resort **Štrbské Pleso** (red markers) or to the mountain railway stop **Popradské pleso**.

4 Vodopád Skok, 1750 m

Through the sunny valley to the vodopád Skok waterfall

Štrbské Pleso – Mlynická dolina – Skok – Pleso nad Skokom

Location: Štrbské Pleso, 1355 m.
Starting point: Last stop on the mountain railway Štrbské Pleso. Car park near the last stop.
Walking times: From the last railway stop to the lake 10 min., from there into the valley to the waterfall 1¼ hrs., to the small lake above the waterfall another 20 min. The descent takes 1¼ hrs. Total walking time 3 to 4 hrs.
Grade: Up to the upper forest edge, a well-maintained path, further along a walkway partially covered in gravel. Along the lake wall above the waterfall, the path is secured with chains.
Highest point: Pleso nad Skokom, 1801 m.
Refreshments/Accommodation: Only at the start of the valley, the Hotel FIS and at the valley station of the chairlift in the ski centre.

The tour leads past Štrbské pleso. The view from the southwestern shore of this lake of the peaks of the Tatra is one of the most beautiful in the High Tatra.

From the **last stop** on the mountain railway, go to the department store, head up on the stairs to the right, over the road and between the trees to the southeastern shore of the **lake**. Because of the grand panoramas, we recommend making a short side-trip of about 200 m to the southwestern shore. Continue on a yellow-markered path in a northerly direction. Walking through the forest, we reach the signpost on the main path. From here, following the yellow markers, we head steadily north to the ski centre in the forest. After ¾ hr., the path leads out of the forest and moderately ascends in open terrain to the waterfall. Experienced hikers can walk up along the left edge of the lake wall to the higher valley terrace, to the smaller lake above the waterfall. This section is secured with chains in two places. **Return** along the same route.

On the path to the Skok waterfall. The Štrbský štít peak in the background.

5 Predné Solisko, 2093 m

A panoramic summit in the vicinity of the chairlift

Štrbské Pleso – Chata pod Soliskom – Predné Solisko

Location: Štrbské Pleso, 1355 m.
Starting point: Last stop of the mountain railway Štrbské Pleso.
Parking: Car park next to the last railway stop.
Walking times: From the last railway stop to the ski centre to the chairlift ¼ hr. Travel with the chairlift 20 min., ascent to summit ¾ hr.; descent through the Furkotská dolina valley to the spa town of Štrbské Pleso 2 hrs. Total walking time 3 hrs.
Grade: From the Chata pod Soliskom hut, the ascent to the summit Predné Solisko is via a finished path. Descent through the Furkotská dolina valley also on a finished walkway, to the spa town Štrbské Pleso along a forest trail. The tour is marked.
Highest point: Predné Solisko, 2093 m.
Refreshments/Accommodation: The Bivak Club at the summit station of the chairlift and the Chata pod Soliskom hut, 1830 m.

Predné Solisko is the first and lowest summit in the long mountain ridge between the Furkotská and Mlynická dolina valleys, which ends in the Bystré sedlo saddle.
From the mountain railway station, head north along the road to the ski centre and ride up the mountain on the chairlift. From the **top station** of the chairlift, walk along the red-waymarked path above the hut and further along serpentine curves above a grassy slope up to the **ridge**. Follow the ridge up to the **summit**.
The **descent** is only safe along the ascent route! The seemingly easy terrain which entices the hiker directly to the Furkotská dolina valley is very steep in its lower portions. A descent along that route takes longer than the return to the hut. From the hut, continue along the blue-markered path to the signpost in the **valley floor** (20 min.) and along the yellow-markered walkway downhill to a forest trail ending in the town of **Štrbské Pleso**.

The Predné Solisko, and behind it, the snowy peak of the Štrbské Solisko.

6 Bystrá lávka, 2300 m

Around two valleys

Štrbské Pleso – Chata pod Soliskom – Furkotská dolina – Bystrá lávka – Mlynická dolina – Štrbské Pleso

Location: Štrbské Pleso, 1355 m.
Starting point: The Chata pod Soliskom hut, 1830 m. Arrive here from Štrbské Pleso with the chairlift in 20 min.
Parking: Car park near the last stop of the mountain railway.
Walking times: From the Chata pod Soliskom hut to the Furkotská dolina valley, 20 min.; through the valley to the Bystrá lávka wind gap, 2 hrs.; descent through Mlynická dolina valley 2½ hrs.; total walking time 5 hrs.
Grade: From the Chata pod soliskom hut, a well-maintained walkway to the upper lake in Furkotská dolina valley. Further along a newly-constructed walkway to the gap, the last 10 m are secured with chains. On the descent, a short section secured with chains beneath the gap. Further on a well-maintained walkway. The tour is marked.
Highest point: Bystrá lávka, 2300 m.
Refreshments/Accommodation: The Chata pod Soliskom hut.

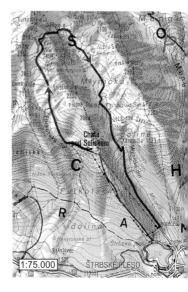

Bystrá lávka is a narrow wind gap on the northern end of the Solisko ridge – it provides an easy passageway between the Mlynická and Furkotská dolina valleys. On the shady scree-covered slopes beneath the gap, the firn fields can last into the summer months and make the crossing more difficult. If there is only snow on the northern side, that is, along the descent route, we recommend returning to the starting point via the ascent route. The old walkway through the Bystré sedlo saddle (this gap is located on the same ridge, however about 200 m north of the Bystrá lávka, directly beneath the summit of the Furkotská štít) was closed by the TANAP administration in 1993.

From the **hut**, head along the blue-markered path in a westerly direction along a moderate descent path into **Furkotská dolina** valley and to the signpost, 1710 m. Continue on the yellow-markered path uphill, over grassy meadows and between mountain pines. Hike along serpentines over a rock

Bystrá lávka (left) and Furkotský štít from the east.

moraine and two valley swells into the valley basin and to the upper lake. Here, the new path leaves the valley floor and proceeds to the right uphill to the lowest point in the ridge. You can also ascend from Mlynická dolina valley, which is prettier, but more difficult, since you cannot use the chairlift.

On the **descent** into **Mlynická dolina** valley, you soon reach an old pathway which leads past two lakes and the Skok waterfall to the valley station of the chairlift.

7 Satan, 2416 m

Where the devil calls home

Štrbské Pleso – Mlynická dolina – Volie plieska – Satan

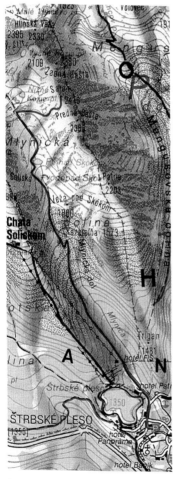

Location: Štrbské Pleso, 1355 m.
Starting point: Last stop of the mountain railway Štrbské Pleso.
Parking: Car park next to the mountain railway stop.
Walking Times: Through the Mlynická dolina valley 2 hrs.; from the Volie plieska lakes beneath the wall ¼ hr.; ascent to the summit 2 hrs.; descent along the same route 3 hrs. Total walking time 7 to 8 hrs.
Grade: Through the Mlynická dolina valley along a marked trail, further up, a mountain path. From the Volie plieska lakes over boulders (pedestrian terrain) up to the point beneath the wall. Some spots have Difficulty Grade I. Only permitted in the company of a mountain guide!
Highest point: Satan, 2416 m.
Refreshments/Accommodation: Only at the entry to the valley at Hotel FIS and at the valley station of the chairlift.

The mighty Satan is the highest peak in the Bašty mountain crest, which separates the valleys Mlynická dolina and Menusovská dolina. It got its name several hundred years ago, when, on its slopes, treasure-hunters wandered around, often threatened by falling rocks. According to an old legend, Satan and other devils protect the treasures hidden within the mountains in this way.

From the **last stop of the mountain railway,** take the road to the north in the direction of the ski centre, and continue along the yellow-markered path uphill through Mlynická dolina valley.

The rocky peaks of Satan, Zadná Bastá, Capie veže and Hlinská veža.

Walk along the mountain path at the **Skok** waterfall, past **Pleso nad Skokom** lake, and over the valley narrows to the further terrace. The mountain path now leads between two lakes: the **Volle plieska** lakes, at which our tour takes a new direction. Head right (to the east) over the rocky ridge beneath the southwestern face of Satan. Its five steep gullies can be crossed over a small belt. On the belt to the second-to-last gully, head up and cross over to the last gully – that one being on the **southern summit**.

The **descent** either follows the ascent route or heads along the southeastern crest to the saddle above the Široký žľab gully. Orientation is somewhat difficult on the circumvention of the Predná Bašta summit. Continue further along a scree-covered slope of the Malá Bašta in a southwesterly direction into Mlynická dolina valley, and through it, back to the starting point.

8 Popradské pleso, 1494 m

To the lake in the heart of the mountains

Štrbské Pleso – Trigan – Popradské pleso – Symbolický cintorín

Location: Štrbské Pleso, 1355 m.
Starting point: Last stop of the mountain railway Štrbské Pleso. Car park near the railway station.
Walking Times: Trigan 35 min.; to Popradské pleso 40 min.; to the Symbolický cintorín ¼ hr.; descent to the Popradské pleso railway station 50 min. Total walking time 2½ hrs.
Grade: Well-maintained mountain pathway over the Trigan, with portions having steeper ascents to the cemetery, from the fork to the station, an access road.
Highest point: Trigan fork, about 1500 m.
Refreshments/Accommodation: Chata Podpradské pleso hut.

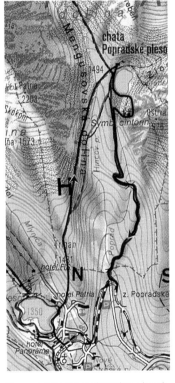

The Popradské pleso is situated in the picturesque valley basin below the mouth of the valley Zlomisková dolina. It is almost 7 hectares large, and reaches a depth of 18 m.

From the **last stop** of the mountain railway, head along the road about 500 m in a northerly direction. Continue to the right, as seen from the signpost, following the red markers; behind the bridge, a mountain pathway branches off of the street to the left into the forest, which leads in a constant ascent to the fork on **Trigan**. Here, a green-markered mountain path branches off, heading downhill; this path is suitable for tours in winter. Our route, however, continues along the red-markered path, past the rocky cliff, and gradually ascends into the Mengusovská dolina valley, and down to Popradské pleso lake. From the **shelter**, continue on the yellow-markered path along the southwestern lake shore, to the **cemetery**. Continue on the path, whose descent becomes steeper, and over the stream onto the road. From the station of the Popradské pleso mountain railway, you can return to Štrbské Pleso by train or on foot (20 min. on the very quiet road).

Chapel at the Symbolic Cemetery near Popradské pleso.

9 Veľké Hincovo pleso, 1946 m, Kôprovský štít, 2367 m

To the largest lake on the southern slope of the High Tatra

Popradské pleso – Veľké Hincovo pleso – Kôprovský štít

Location: Štrbské Pleso, 1355 m.
Starting point: Railway stop of the Popradské pleso mountain railway, 1250 m.
Parking: Near the railway stop.
Walking Times: To Popradské pleso 1 hr.; on to Veľké Hincovo pleso 1½ hrs.; to Vyšné Kôprovské sedlo ½ hr.; to Kôprovský štít ¾ hrs.; descent 3¼ hrs. Total walking time 7 hrs.

Grade: Mountain path to the saddle, from there to the summit, at the start, on remnants of a path, then between boulders. Along the ridge there is rocky terrain. The tour is marked.
Highest points: Vyšné Kôprovské sedlo, 2180 m, Kôprovský štít, 2367 m.
Refreshments/Accommodation: The hut chata Porpradské pleso.

The Veľké Hincovo pleso is the fourth-largest lake in the High Tatra, with an area of 20 hectares, a depth of 53 m and a length of 740 m. The rocky Kôprovský štít, an elongated mountain peak, situated northwest of the lake,

The Kôprovský štít and lake Veľké Hincovo pleso.

sinks down to the Vyšné Kôprovské sedlo with an entirely gentle slope, through which our tour runs. From the summit, there is an interesting view, primarily of the mountains Rysy and Vysoká.

From the railway station of the mountain railway **Popradské pleso**, head along a car-free road to the north (blue markers) to the fork above the lake. Continue uphill through **Mengusovská dolina** valley (blue markers) to the turnoff in the direction of Rysy. Here, go to the left over the Hincov potok stream (be careful if the water level is high!), and up, more steeply, over two hills, into the valley basin of the **Hincove plesá** lakes. From the largest lake, at the signpost, go left and follow the steep serpentine curves up to the **Vyšné Kôprovské sedlo** saddle. The route forks at this point; the blue markers lead into the Hlinská dolina valley, and our tour, following the red markers, leads over a grassy slope in a northwesterly direction up to the edge of the slope. Behind it, the ascent direction turns to the northeast, and leads between boulders up to the ridge. The trail disappears in spots, but the red markers lead reliably to the preliminary summit, and after the wind gap, ultimately to the **summit**, following along the ridge.

The **descent** follows the same route to the Vyšné Kôprovské sedlo saddle, and from there, through the valley Hlinská dolina or, on a shorter route, through the valley Mengusovská dolina.

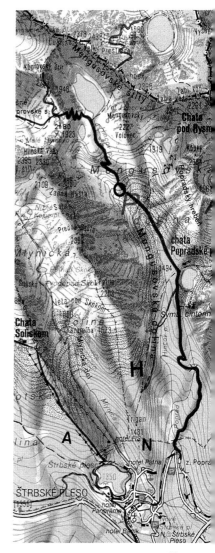

10 Mengusovské sedlo, 2307 m, and Východný Mengusovský štít, 2398 m

On the trail of Polish poachers

Popradské pleso – Veľké Hincovo pleso – Mengusovské sedlo and Východný Mengusovský štít

Location: Štrbské Pleso, 1355 m.
Starting point: Railway stop of the mountain railway Popradské pleso, 1250 m.
Parking: Next to the railway stop of the mountain railway.
Walking Times: Popradské pleso 1 hr.; on to Veľké Hincovo pleso 1½ hrs.; to the saddle, 1 hr.; on to the summit 1 hr.; descent 3½ hrs. Total walking time 8 hrs.
Grade: Up to the Veľké Hincovo pleso lake a maintained, marked mountain pathway,

further on, walking terrain with a short section having Difficulty Grade I. From the saddle to the summit, also sections in Difficulty Grade I., as well as difficult orientation. The last section requires the use of a safety rope. Only permitted in the company of a mountain guide!
Highest point: The saddle Mengusovské sedlo, 2307 m, the summit Východný Mengusovský štít, 2398 m.
Refreshments/Accommodation: The hut chata Popradské pleso.

The saddle Mengusovské sedlo and the peak of Východný Mengusovský štít.

In the mighty face of the peaks of Mengusovské štíty, there seems to be no accessible path on first inspection. However, this face does have its weak spot: From the large cone of detritus under the southern wall of Východný Mengusovský štít, a cleft in the cliff runs diagonally to the left and upwards, which, farther up, becomes a ramp which gets wider and wider under the Mengusovské sedlo saddle. Our route leads through this cleft, along which poachers from Podhalie had climbed to the southern valleys of the High Tatra for ages. The fourth-largest mountain lake in the High Tatra, the Veľké Hincovo pleso, is an inviting spot for a rest.

A blue-markered route leads from the railway stop of the mountain railway **Popradské pleso** to lake **Veľké Hincovo pleso** (see Tour 9).

From the southern shore of the mountain lake (signposted), head in a northeasterly direction to the moraine slope (remnants of a trail), to the large cone of detritus, and following the trail on, to the mouth of the cleft in the cliff wall, which leads down to the left from the summit.

Head under the mouth to the left onto the ramp and through the cleft, which crosses a few side gullies, up to the **saddle**.

The ascent from the saddle to the summit does not lead along the northwestern ridge, but rather, along the southern slopes. By crossing a long line of rocky ribs, we reach the summit, and along it, arrive at the **summit**. The **descent** follows the same route.

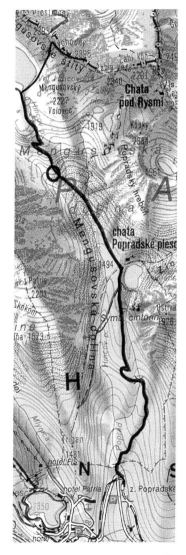

11 Rysy, 2499 m

To the summit with the best vista of the High Tatra

Popradské pleso – Žabie plesá – sedlo Váha – Rysy

Rysy with the Váha saddle and the ascent path.

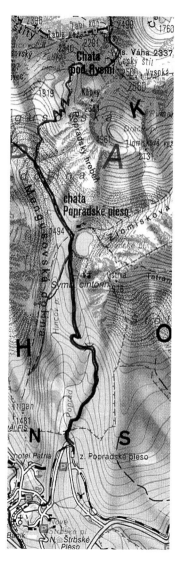

Location: Štrbské Pleso, 1355 m
Starting point: Railway stop of the mountain railway Popradské pleso, 1250 m.
Parking: Next to the railway stop.
Walking Times: Popradské pleso 1 hr.; on to Žabie plesá 1½ hrs.; to Chata pod Rysmi 1 hr.; from sedlo Váha hut to sedlo Váha 1/4 hr.; and on to Rysy ½ hr.; descent 3½ hrs. Total walking time 8 hrs.
Grade: A finished mountain path leads to the Chata pod Rysmi hut. The entire tour is marked, and one spot is secured with chains.
Highest points: The saddle sedlo Váha 2337 m, Rysy, 2499 m.
Refreshments/Accommodation: Chata Popradské pleso cabin, Chata pod Rysmi hut.

Rysy is a double-peaked mountain, whose northwestern peak forms the hub of three mountain ridges. From the summit, there is a wonderful panorama of the mountains and valleys of the High Tatra. The most impressive is the view of the two large Polish lakes Czarny Staw and Morskie Oko in the northwest.

From the railway stop of the mountain railway **Popradské pleso**, head north, following the blue markers, to Mengusovská dolina valley up to the fork over the Žabí potok stream, 1625 m. Here, a red-markered mountain pathway branches off, which leads to the valley basin of the **Žabie plesá** lakes on a serpentine path via the valley swell. A further swell, where the only difficult spot is secured with chains, leads to the valley **Dolinka pod Váhou** and past the hut, up to the saddle. Continue on the southern side beneath the mountain crest to the **summit**.

The **descent** can only be undertaken on the ascent route.

12 Vysoká, 2560 m

The most beautiful summit of the High Tatra

Popradské pleso – sedlo Váha – Vysoká – Dračie sedlo – Popradské pleso

Location: Štrbské Pleso, 1355 m.
Starting point: Railway stop of the mountain railway Popradské pleso, 1250 m.
Parking: Next to the railway stop.
Walking Times: To the saddle sedlo Váha 3¾ hrs.; from here up to the summit 2 hrs.; descent into the saddle Dracie sedlo 1¼ hrs.; through Zlomisková dolina valley to Lake Popradské pleso 1¾ hrs.; to the railway stop ¾ hr. Total walking time 10 hrs.
Grade: Mountain pathway to the saddle sedlo Váha. Ascent to the summit in rocky terrain (partially Grade I), without markers. Difficult sections secured with chains and cramps. Only permitted in the company of a mountain guide!
Highest points: The saddle sedlo Váha, 2337 m, Vysoká, 2560 m, the saddle Dracie sedlo, 2200 m.
Refreshments/Accommodation: The chata Popradské pleso hut, the Chata pod Rysmi hut.

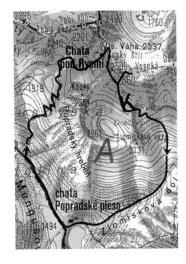

The Vysoká, a mountain with four peaks, is situated in the main crest between the saddle sedlo Váha and Zlomisková dolina valley. The most beautiful view of Vysoká can be seen from the climatic health resort Štrbské Pleso: The two highest peaks are framed on the left by Český štít, 2500 m, and the right by Dračí štít, 2523 m. All four peaks together form the crown of the Vysoká. The tour is easier to walk when there is no snow in the main gully. From the mountain railway stop **Popradské pleso**, head to the saddle sedlo Váha (see Tour 11). From the saddle, initially walk along the northwestern crest of the mountain **Český štít**, then straight across its western face on the upper of the two belts to a point beyond the peak's fall line. Head through the chimney uphill (there are chains), into the wind gap under the **Kohútik** tower, and on the other side of the ridge, over the banks of detritus into the main gully of the Vysoká. Through this gully, ultimately head left (secured) and onto the **northwest summit**. The **descent** also follows the main gully to the bank of detritus, and on over the right slope between boulders. Finally, traverse the Dracie sedlo saddle and turn left to Zlomisková dolina valley.

On Štrbské pleso lake, the snowy Vysoká in the background.

13 Východná Železná brána, 2255 m

Into the wildest valley basin of the mountain range

Popradské pleso – Ľadové pleso – Východná Železná brána – Kačacia dolina – Lysá poľana

Location: Štrbské Pleso, 1355 m.
Starting point: Railway stop of the mountain railway Popradské pleso, 1250 m (car park).
Walking times: Popradské pleso 1 hr.; on to Ľadové pleso 1½ hrs.; to the Východná Železná brána saddle 1 hr.; descent into the Kačacia dolina valley to the Zelené Kačacie pleso 2 hrs.; from there to Lysá poľana 2½ hrs.; Total walking time 8 hrs.
Grade: Very long, unmarked mountain tour. A mountain path leads from Popradské pleso lake, and from the Východná Železná brána saddle, a detritus-covered slope. From the saddle, it is difficult (partially Grade I) to Zelené Kačacie pleso lake. Further: marked mountain path, forest trail. Only permitted in the company of a mountain guide!
Highest point: Východná Železná brána, 2255 m, optional: Snežná kopa, 2310 m.
Refreshments/Accommodation: The chata Popradské pleso hut, the guesthouse in the border town Lysá poľana.

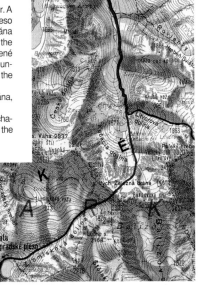

Východná Železná brána is the deepest saddle in the crest, which closes the wild, romantic Valley Zlomisková dolina.

From the railway stop of the mountain railway **Popradské pleso**, head along the access road in a northerly direction (blue markers) to Popradské pleso lake. From the **hut**, head east through Zlomisková dolina valley and over its

The Východná Železná brána saddle. To the left, the Snežná kopa.

three terraces to the **Východná Železná brána** saddle. The rest of the route depends on the snow conditions: If the gully that leans to the north is covered by snow and one thus cannot descend into the Kačacia dolina valley, you can climb up along the southeastern crest to the nearby Snežná kopa summit (20 min.; partially Grade I terrain), and return via the same route.

The **descent** from the saddle to the north is difficult. There is no pathway, and good knowledge of the terrain is required for proper orientation. The tour leads through a wild, deserted valley surrounded by rocky ribs and steep walls, and on Gerlachovské spády slopes to the quiet lake amidst the grassy Kacacia dolina valley. Not far from the lake, you can find the blue-markered pathway into Bielovodská dolina valley. There are bus connections from **Lysá poľana** back to the starting point.

14 Končistá, 2535 m

A mountain crest with ten towers

Popradské pleso – Ľadové pleso – Lúčne sedlo – Končistá

Location: Štrbské Pleso, 1355 m.
Starting point: Railway stop of the mountain railway Popradské pleso, 1250 m.
Parking: Near the railway stop of the mountain railway.
Walking times: Popradské pleso 1 hr.; on to Ľadové pleso 1½ hrs.; to Lúčne sedlo 1 hr.; to the summit a further 1½ hrs.; descent via the Ostrva 4 hrs. Total walking time 9 hrs.
Grade: From Popradské pleso lake, a non-

maintained pathway leads to the Zlomisková dolina valley, from Ľadové pleso lake over scree and moraine slopes to the summit. Strenuous, unmarked tour, but no rock-climbing spots. Only permitted in the company of a mountain guide!
Highest point: The Končistá summit, 2535 m.
Refreshments/Accommodation: The chata Popradské pleso hut.

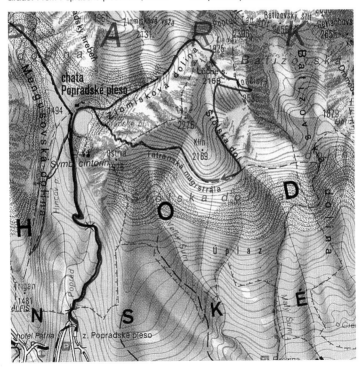

Panorama of the Lúčne sedlo saddle, Končistá and Gerlachovský štít.

On its eastern side, the Končistá has a sheer face which plunges down to the east, and has two peaks closely packed together: The southern peak is the main peak, and is formed by a strange boulder that looks something like a horse's head. The lower northern peak is the destination of typical ascents.

From the **Popradské pleso** railway stop, head north along the access road (blue markers) to Popradské pleso lake. From the hut, travel through Zlomisková dolina valley to **Ľadové pleso** lake. Turn right onto the scree-covered slope, and head uphill in a southerly direction beneath the **Lúčne sedlo** saddle. A rocky step is located beneath the saddle, which is difficult to traverse, and over which water usually runs. However, the mountain guides know how to get around this obstacle, which is the only one on this tour. In the saddle, our direction switches to the southeast. The route follows the actual ascent over a monotonous, scree-covered slope up to the ridge, which is accessible in the **wind gap** between the southern and northern peaks of the Koncistá.

The **descent** follows the same route up to the Lúcne sedlo saddle; then, we turn to the south through the **Stôlska dolina** valley, which can be crossed farther downward via a red-markered pathway. On this path, we then walk to the west over the Sedlo pod Ostrvou saddle to **Popradské pleso** lake, or, even shorter, to the east and further beneath the fork, which is situated at the foot of the Koncistá, on the yellow-markered pathway to Vyšné Hágy.

15 Ostrva, 1980 m

A sunny vista over Popradské pleso lake

Štrbské Pleso – Popradské pleso – Ostrva – Batizovské pleso – Tatranská Polianka

Location: Štrbské Pleso, 1355 m.
Starting point: Last stop of the Štrbské Pleso mountain railway.
Parking: Car park next to the railway station.
Walking times: Štrbské Pleso – Popradské pleso 1¼ hrs.; to the Sedlo pod Ostrvou saddle 1 hr.; on to the Ostrva summit 5 min.; to Batizovské pleso 1½ hrs.; descent to Tatranská Polianka 1¾ hrs. Total walking time 5½ hrs.

Grade: This mountain tour runs along a finished and marked mountain pathway, the last section along an access road.
Highest points: The Sedlo pod Ostrvou saddle, 1959 m, Ostrva summit 1980 m, Lake Batizovské pleso 1879 m.
Refreshments/Accommodation: The chata Popradské pleso hut.

The Ostrva is situated at the end of the branching crest of the Tupá. There are a few eagle's eyries within the difficult to reach rock walls. At the foot of the mountain, groups of old Swiss pines, and the symbolic mountain climbers' cemetery, can be found.

From the last railway stop, Štrbské Pleso, head north on the road for about 500 m to the sign and, as in

Tour 8, go right on the red-markered pathway to lake **Popradské pleso**; switch to the eastern lake shore in front of the hut. Here, head left and up along 30 serpentine curves, each one more steep than the last, until you reach the **saddle**. After a short turn-off to the highest point of the **Ostrva**, we continue our tour horizontally, along the southern slope of the mountains Tupá and Klin, and along the foot of the Koncistá to lake **Batizovské pleso**. From the fork below the Suchý vrch hill, 1720 m, go downhill on the yellow-markered path into **Velická dolina** and on the traffic-free road to Tatranská Polianka. **Return** to the starting point via the mountain railway.

The Ostrva, as seen from lake Popradské pleso.

16 Batizovské pleso, 1879 m

To the lake at the foot of the highest Tatra peak.

Vyšné Hágy – Batizovské pleso – Sliezsky dom – Tatranská Polianka

Location: Vyšné Hágy, 1100 m.
Starting point: The Vyšné Hágy mountain railway station.
Parking: Car park next to the street to Štrbské Pleso, 400 m away from the crossing in the centre of town.
Walking times: Batizovské pleso 2 hrs.; on to Sliezsky dom 1 hr.; descent to Tatranská

Polianka 1½ hrs. Total walking time 4½ hrs.
Grade: Maintained pathway, parts of which are steep. The entire tour is marked.
Highest point: Lake Batizovské pleso, 1879 m.
Refreshments/Accommodation: Mountain hotel Sliezsky dom.

The Batizovské pleso is the lowest-situated lake in Batizovská pleso valley. It is located behind a moraine wall that separates the valley. The lake has no visible feeder stream, but the stream Batizovský potok rises from it, which

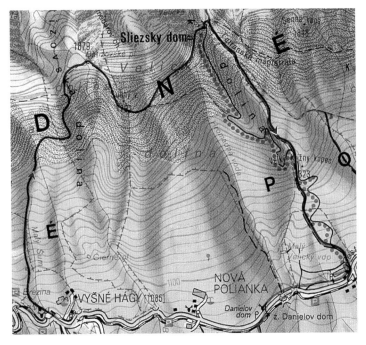

Lake Batizovské pleso with the peak of the Batizovský štít.

forms three waterfalls that can be seen from our path. From the **Vyšné Hágy** mountain railway station, head west (yellow markers) down to the road – opposite the car park on the other side – and to the right, on a gravel-covered forest trail over the railway tracks to the **forester's house**. Further up, the forest trail forks several times; pay attention to the markers! Starting from the open shelter in a meadow, head right on the path. After passing two steep uphill stretches, go over the **Batizovská Suchá voda** stream and, behind it, head over a slope with Swiss mountain pines, to the sign at the foot of the Koncistá. Following the red markers, continue above lake **Batizovské pleso**, and over the southern slopes of the Gerlachovský kotol basin to the mountain hotel **Sliezsky dom**. The **descent** follows the green-markered trail to Tatranská Polianka. Return to the starting point by train or bus.

17 Sliezsky dom, 1670 m

Walk to the mountain hotel on Lake Velické pleso

Tatranská Polianka – Velická dolina – Gerlachovský hrebeň – Sliezsky dom

Location: Tatranská Polianka, 1000 m.
Starting point: At the signpost in the centre of town.
Parking: On the side street in the direction of Svit, beneath the railway tracks; a larger car park is located along the main road, 400 m west of the town.
Walking times: Tatranská Polianka – Sliezsky dom 2½ hrs.; descent 2 hrs. Total walking time 4½ hrs.
Grade: Moderately ascending road closed to public traffic.
Highest point: The mountain hotel Sliezsky dom, 1670 m.
Refreshments/Accommodation: Mountain hotel Sliezsky dom.

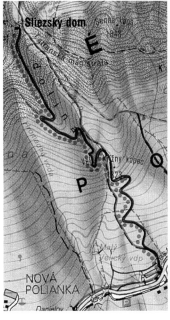

The mountain hotel Sliezsky dom is situated on the southern shore of the small lake Velické pleso. From above, the stream Velický potok flows down and into the lake in the form of a waterfall. A walking path circles the lake; benches are located at the end of this path.

From **Tatranská Polianka**, follow the green-markered access road past the tennis courts and into the forest, where the path moderately rises in a curve, in which the green markers branch off to the left on a non-maintained path that, although it leads us directly to our destination, is very steep. Our route leads through several curves to the sign at the **Velický most** bridge, 1304 m, crosses the green-markered path, and leads over the bridge to the other bank of the Velický potok stream. Following along the slope of the **Gerlachovský hrebeň** mountain crest, we arrive, after taking five curves, at an open mountain slope with a view to the Granátové veže mountain group and the Slavkovský štít. After two more curves, the yellow marker points to the left. It follows the last section with a view to the Velická dolina valley and to the mountain hotel **Sliezsky dom**, where the road ends. The **return** route follows the ascent route.

The mountain hotel Sliezsky dom.

18 Poľský hrebeň, 2200 m, and Východná Vysoká, 2428 m

A rocky pyramid towering over three valleys

Starý Smokovec – Velická dolina – Dlhé pleso – Poľský hrebeň – Východná Vysoká

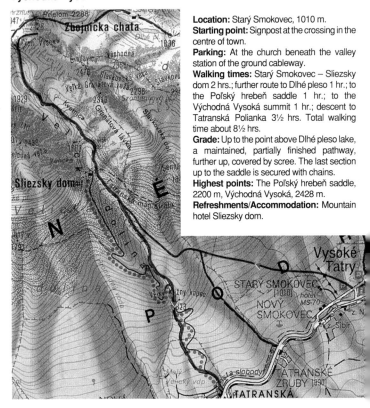

Location: Starý Smokovec, 1010 m.
Starting point: Signpost at the crossing in the centre of town.
Parking: At the church beneath the valley station of the ground cableway.
Walking times: Starý Smokovec – Sliezsky dom 2 hrs.; further route to Dlhé pleso 1 hr.; to the Poľský hrebeň saddle 1 hr.; to the Východná Vysoká summit 1 hr.; descent to Tatranská Polianka 3½ hrs. Total walking time about 8½ hrs.
Grade: Up to the point above Dlhé pleso lake, a maintained, partially finished pathway, further up, covered by scree. The last section up to the saddle is secured with chains.
Highest points: The Poľský hrebeň saddle, 2200 m, Východná Vysoká, 2428 m.
Refreshments/Accommodation: Mountain hotel Sliezsky dom.

The valley basin of Velické pleso lake is enclosed by a swell to the north, over which a waterfall flows. To the right of the waterfall, our pathway leads underneath overhanging rocks to the Poľský hrebeň saddle.

The Poľský hrebeň saddle, and behind it, the Prielom saddle and the Východná Vysoká peak.

From the Východná Vysoká summit, we have a wide panorama, especially of the Veľká Studená dolina valley.

From the signpost in **Starý Smokovec**, head between the houses (yellow markers) and across the street, and further on, over the meadow with a ski lift and through woods into the **Velická dolina** valley. Continue, following the green markers in a northwesterly direction up the valley, past Velické pleso lake, over the steps of the waterfall and above **Dlhé pleso** lake to the end of the valley. The path ends here. A belt of rocks follows, interrupted through a few steps, secured by chains, which leads to the **Poľský hrebeň** saddle. From the saddle, head to the right, in a northeasterly direction, on a yellow-markered mountain pathway to the **summit**.

The **return** to the saddle can only be undertaken on the same route. From the Poľský hrebeň saddle, you can return to the **Sliezscky dom** mountain hotel and reach **Tatranská Polianka** via the green-markered path, which represents the shortest descent route. A longer and more strenuous return route from the Poľský hrebeň saddle leads over the **Prielom** saddle (see Tour 23) and through the Veľká Studená dolina valley to the ground cableway at **Hrebienok**.

19 Gerlachovský štít, 2655 m

Through gorges and over rocks to the highest summit of the High Tatra

Tatranská Polianka – Sliezcky dom – Gerlachovský štít – Batizovské pleso

The Gerlachovský štít is situated in the middle of the High Tatra. In the south, it is characterized by a striking rocky basin, which makes it easy to spot among the other mountains when viewed from the Poprad valley basin. For a long time, the summit was considered insurmountable, and until the year 1838, no one even knew that it was the highest peak of the High Tatra.

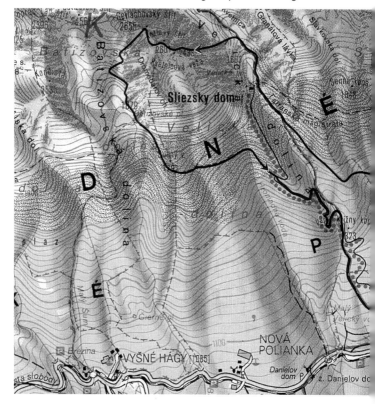

Location: Tatranská Polianka, 1000 m.
Starting point: The Sliezsky dom mountain hotel, 1670 m. From Tatranská Polianka (green markers), it is accessible in 2 hrs. or from Starý Smokovec (yellow markers) in 2 hrs.
Parking: In Tatranská Polianka, on the side street in the direction of Svit.
Walking times: Sliezsky dom – Gerlachovský štít 4 hrs.; descent to Batizovské pleso 2½ hrs. The entire hike including return to Tatranská Polianka lasts 10 – 11 hrs.

Grade: This tour is one of the most difficult mountain hikes in the High Tatra. A great difference in elevation must be surmounted! The terrain is mostly without a trail, and very rocky; several sections of it are Difficulty Grade I; the exposed spots are secured with chains. Complicated orientation, since there are no markers! Only permitted in the company of a mountain guide!
Highest point: Gerlachovský štít, 2655 m.
Refreshments/Accommodation: Hotel Sliezsky dom.

From the hotel **Sliezsky dom**, follow the green-markered pathway over the steps of the waterfall **Velický vodopád**. Head over the stream and onto the unmarked pathway under the mouth of the gully **Velický žľab**. At the wall to the right of the mouth, hike uphill, with the aid of the chain handrails, and along the gully to the ridge. Continue from the first wind gap above the basin to a further wind gap in the southwest ridge. From here, you can already see the summit. Through broken country over several gullies into the upper portion of the **Batizovský žľab** gorge, and beyond it to the summit. From the summit along the ascent route back to the second gully. Here downhill into the Batizovský žľab gorge, which ends in a 100-m high wall. This wall can be bypassed via the so-called »**Batizovská próba**« (chains). Beneath the wall along the pathway to the southwest, to **Batizovské pleso**. Follow the red markers to the signpost under the Suchý vrch rise. From here, take the yellow-markered trail into Velická dolina, and then follow the green markers to **Tatranská Polianka**.

The Gerlachovský štít peak. To the left, the peak of Zadný Gerlachovský štít,....

... to the right, the three-pronged tower of the Çertova veža.

20 Bradavica, 2476 m

A mountain with four peaks

Hrebienok – Sliezsky dom – Kvetnica – Bradavica

Location: Starý Smokovec, 1010 m.
Starting point: Hrebienok, top station of the ground cableway from Starý Smokovec, 1280 m. Holiday home, restaurant, ski lifts.
Parking: At the church below the valley station of the ground cableway.
Walking times: Hrebienok – mountain hotel Sliezsky dom 2 hrs.; further on to Kvetnica ¾ hrs.; ascent to the Bradavica summit 2¼ hrs.; descent to Sliezsky dom mountain hotel 2 hrs.; further on to Starý Smokovec 2 hrs. Total walking time 9 hrs.

Grade: A finished, marked pathway leads into the Kvetnica valley basin. The tour continues through steep walking terrain with portions having the Difficulty Grade I, no markers. In the upper portion, the mountain tour is exposed; depending on the conditions, a safety rope is necessary. Only permitted in the company of a mountain guide!
Highest point: The Bradavica summit, 2476 m.
Refreshments/Accommodation: Mountain hotel Sliezsky dom.

Looking up at Bradavica mountain from the Velická dolina valley, the mountain has the shape of a low cylinder with four peaks. The highest is the

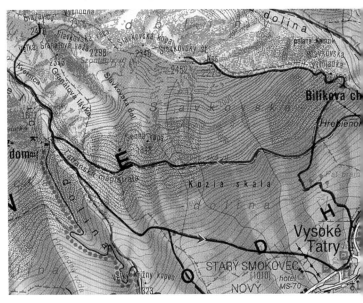

The Granátové veže crest, to the left the Bradavica peak.

northeast peak, but the eastern peak, almost as high, is the typical destination of mountain hikers. There is also a summit book there.

From the **top station** of the ground cableway, walk along the red-markered pathway in a westerly direction over the mountain slope of Slavkovský štít and beneath the mouth of the Slavskovská dolina valley to the signpost at the mountain hotel **Sliezsky dom**. Continue to the right (green markers), over the steps with the waterfall and into the **Kvetnica** valley basin. The ascent route is determined by the southwest gorge of the Bradavica summit. Its lower portion is interrupted by inaccessible steps in a few places, and the upper portion leads under the Kvetnicové sedlo saddle and into a vertical chimney. Both parts are bypassed via terrain which, in terms of climbing, is not difficult, but which is very difficult in terms of orientation.

The **descent** is usually made following the same route; however, as an exception, if there is no snow in the north gorge, you can continue the tour by descending to the saddle beneath the Kupola summit and on to Dlhé pleso lake.

21 Slavkovský štít, 2452 m

Over a long, rocky crest

Hrebienok – Slavkovská vyhliadka – Nos – Slavkovský štít

Location: Starý Smokovec, 1010 m.
Starting point: Hrebienok, 1280 m, the top station of the ground cableway from Starý Smokovec.
Parking: At the church beneath the valley station of the ground cableway.
Walking times: Hrebienok – Slavkovská vyhliadka ¾ hrs.; further on to the preliminary peak Nos 2¼ hrs.; to Slavkovský štít 1 hr.; descent directly to Starý Smokovec 3 hrs. Total walking time 7 hrs.

Grade: Finished pathway, partially somewhat steep. The entire tour is marked. The mountain crest is very exposed to wind, and in the case of thunderstorms, at risk of being struck by lightning. Only recommended in safe weather conditions!
Highest points: Nos, 2272 m, Slavkovský štít, 2452 m.
Refreshments/Accommodation: None along the route.

Slavkovský štít is an elongated mountain crest possessing two faces. To the southwest, the peak leans with a moderately steep mountain slope, but in the northeast, its mighty cliff walls plunge down almost 1000 metres into Veľká Studená dolina valley. Our route leads along the border of these very different sides, on the south-eastern crest, up to the saddle beyond the preliminary peak Nos.

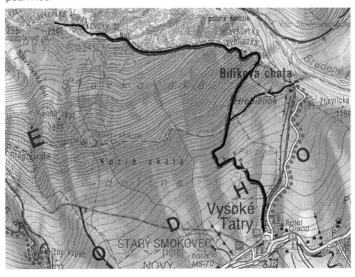

Slavkovský štít, and the southeast crest on the edge of the cloud.

From **Hrebienok**, head west on the red-markered pathway for 20 minutes to the first fork. A blue-markered path leads in from Starý Smokovec, on which we continue our tour to the right, heading uphill up to the **panoramic hill**, Slavkovská vyhliadka (25 min.). Here, the forest ends, and the path initially skirts the crest in a few serpentine curves, until it finally meets the mountain crest. With the exception of two short sections on the northern side, it now steadily leads along the southern side, up to the preliminary peak **Nos**. The last section leads along a wide mountain slope up to the **summit**, which is situated another 500 m from the saddle.

The **descent** follows the same route. From the sign, take the red-markered path directly downhill, and follow the blue markers to the valley station of the ground cableway in **Starý Smokovec**.

22 Zbojnícka chata, 1960 m

Through a picturesque valley to the meadows near six small lakes

Hrebienok – poľana Kamzík – Veľká Studená dolina – Zbojnícka chata

Location: Starý Smokovec, 1010 m.
Starting point: Hrebienok, 1280 m, top station of the ground cableway from the valley town Starý Smokovec. Holiday home, restaurant and ski lifts.
Parking: At the church beneath the valley station of the ground cableway in Starý Smokovec.
Walking times: Hrebienok – Zbojnícka chata

2½ hrs.; descent 2 hrs. Total walking time 4½ hrs.
Grade: Finished pathway with a moderate incline. The entire hike is marked.
Highest point: The Zbojnícka chata hut, 1960 m.
Refreshments/Accommodation: The huts Bilíkova chata and Zbojnícka chata.

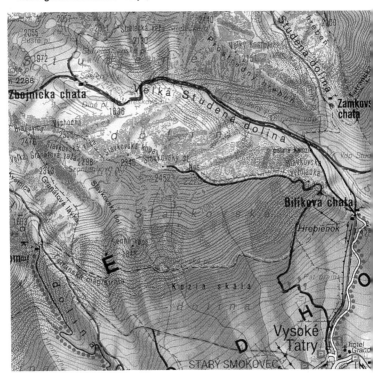

There are six lakes among the meadows in the area surrounding the Zbojnícka chata hut. The most beautiful of them is Starolesnianske pleso lake. It is accessible in 10 minutes from the hut on the yellow-markered pathway. From **Hrebienok**, go northwest on a red-markered path to the intersections of the hiking trails at the mountain meadow **poľana Kamzík**. Watch out for falling rocks! This section can be bypassed via a path next to the waterfalls; green and blue markers, ½ hr. From the intersection, follow the blue-markered trail into **Veľká Studená dolina** valley; after ½ hr., the forest ends. About 20 minutes later, go over a bridge, 1560 m, to the northeastern side of the stream, and further up, cross the valley swell on Brána. Cross back over the stream to the south, and walk steeply for 20 minutes into the valley basin of **Vareškové pleso** lake. Instead of going down to this lake, we now go from here, 1843 m, to the west, heading uphill and up past Dlhé pleso lake to the **hut**.

The **descent** follows the same route.

The Zbojnícka chata hut with Východná Vysoká and the Prielom saddle (centre).

23 Prielom, 2288 m, and Poľský hrebeň, 2200 m

The most interesting mountain hike in the High Tatra

Hrebienok – Zbojnícka chata – Prielom – Poľský hrebeň – Sliezsky dom – Starý Smokovec

Location: Starý Smokovec, 1010 m.
Starting point: Hrebienok, 1280 m, top station of the ground cableway from Starý Smokovec.
Parking: At the church beneath the valley station of the ground cableway to Hrebienok.
Walking times: Hrebienok – Zbojnícka chata 2½ hrs.; further to Prielom 1¼ hrs.; to Poľský hrebeň 1 hr.; Sliezsky dom 1½ hrs.; Starý Smokovec 2 hrs. Total walking time approximately 8 to 9 hrs.
Grade: In the valleys, finished pathways, at the passageways over the Prielom and Poľský hrebeň, there is only a path for parts of the way, the more difficult sections are secured with chains. The entire tour is marked. The hike is only accessible if no snow is present on the steep slopes. You can find out the snow conditions from the mountain service in Starý Smokovec.
Highest points: The Prielom saddle,

2288 m, and the Poľský hrebeň saddle, 2200 m.
Refreshments/Accommodation: The Zbojnícka chata hut and the mountain hotel Sliezsky dom.

From the Prielom mountain saddle, you can enjoy a magnificent view of the striking, approximately 800-m high Gánok north face, as well as Rumanov štít and Zlobivá.

From the **Hrebienok** rise, walk to the Zbojnícka chata hut as described in Tour 22. From the hut, walk along the blue-markered pathway past **Zbojnícke plesá** lake and to the foot of Svišťovy štít into the basin beneath the Divá veža peak. Head over the slope to the right of the gully to the **Prielom** saddle.

The **descent** is made on the other side of the saddle, which is secured with a 20-m long chain. Continue on a scree cone and in serpentine curves into the **Zamrznutý kotol** valley basin. Do not follow the trail all the way to the lake. After a somewhat long crossing at the foot of the northwest face of Východná Vysoká, we arrive at a signpost located beneath the Poľský hrebeň saddle. From that sign, follow the green markers, ultimately walking steeply uphill for ¼ hr. to the **Poľský hrebeň** saddle (crumbling rock!). The **descent** from the Poľský hrebeň saddle into Velická dolina valley: hike over a belt of rocks, interrupted by several steps and secured with chains, in the direction of the scree field at the foot of the southwest slope of Východná Vysoká. Continue on the green-markered path past Dlhé pleso lake and the Sliezsky dom mountain hotel to the Velická poľana meadow, 1562 m.

From here, we continue on a yellow-markered trail to Starý Smokovec.

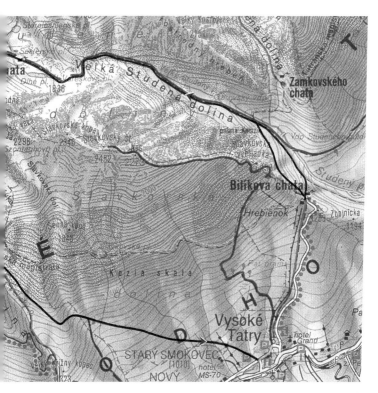

24 Sivé plesá, 2011 m, Strelecká veža, 2130 m

An old hunting spot above the Valley Veľká Studená dolina

Hrebienok – Zbojnícka chata – Sivé plesá – Strelecká veža

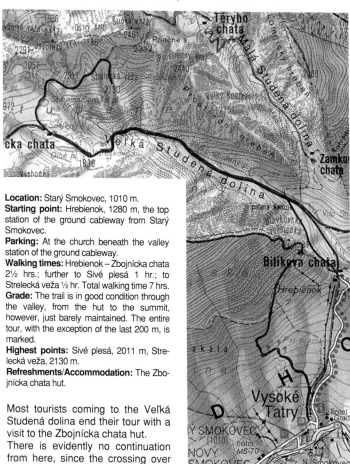

Location: Starý Smokovec, 1010 m.
Starting point: Hrebienok, 1280 m, the top station of the ground cableway from Starý Smokovec.
Parking: At the church beneath the valley station of the ground cableway.
Walking times: Hrebienok – Zbojnícka chata 2½ hrs.; further to Sivé plesá 1 hr.; to Strelecká veža ½ hr. Total walking time 7 hrs.
Grade: The trail is in good condition through the valley, from the hut to the summit, however, just barely maintained. The entire tour, with the exception of the last 200 m, is marked.
Highest points: Sivé plesá, 2011 m, Strelecká veža, 2130 m.
Refreshments/Accommodation: The Zbojnícka chata hut.

Most tourists coming to the Veľká Studená dolina end their tour with a visit to the Zbojnícka chata hut.
There is evidently no continuation from here, since the crossing over the Prielom saddle is considerably

more difficult, and the crossing of the Priečne sedlo saddle is only permitted in the opposite direction. However, within range, there are worthwhile hiking destinations – the Sivé plesá lakes, or the nearby Strelecká veža summit, which rewards us with a wonderful panorama.

Head from the panoramic Hrebienok hill to the Zbojnícka chata hut as described in Tour 22. Walk from the hut to the northwest on the yellow-markered pathway 100 m to the fork. Continue to the right, past the northwest side of the shore of **Sesterské pleso** láke, and over a meadow to Starolesnianske pleso lake. After a moderately steep ascent along the foot of the face of Javorový štít, we arrive at the **Sivé plesá** lakes. Here, the hill between Ostrý štít and Strelecká veža is visible to the northeast. Walk up a few serpentine curves to the hill, and from there, comfortably to the south, on an unmarked path, to the **summit** of Strelecká veža.

The **return** follows the same route. Both valley basins, which surround the tower, are strict nature reserves in which no trespassing is permitted.

The Strelecká veža summit and Ostrý štít (left).

25 Vodopády Stideného potoka, 1250 m

Along waterfalls to the panoramic hill Lomnická vyhliadka

Hrebienok – vodopády – poľana Kamzík – Lomnická – vyhliadka

Location: Starý Smokovec, 1010 m.
Starting point: Hrebienok, 1280 m, the top station of the ground cableway from Starý Smokovec.
Parking: At the church in Starý Smokovec, beneath the valley station of the ground cableway.
Walking Times: Hrebienok – poľana Kamzík ½ hr.; further to Lomnická vyhliadka ¾ hrs.; descent 1 hr. Total walking time 2½ hrs.
Grade: Finished, popular hiking trail; the entire route is marked.
Highest point: Lomnická vyhliadka, 1525 m.
Refreshments/Accommodation: The huts Bilíkova chata, Zamkovského chata (Chata kpt. Nálepku).

The Zamkovského chata hut, in the background the Lomnický hrebeň crest.

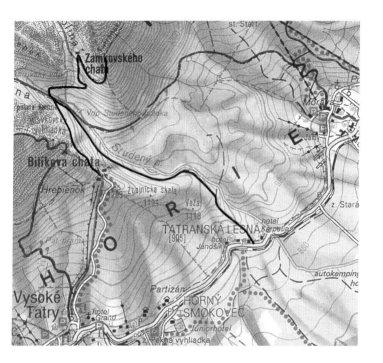

The streams from the two valleys Studené doliny form a row of rather small waterfalls, past which this walk leads.

From the **top station** of the ground cableway on Hrebienok, climb down to the signpost and, on the green-markered pathway, to the Bilíkova chata **hut**. Continue in a steady downward slope along several serpentine curves to the **waterfalls**. From the signpost above the centre waterfall, go uphill on the blue-markered pathway to the mountain meadow **poľana Kamzík**. Now head to the right, on a red-markered trail in front of the giant waterfall to the fork in front of the Zamkovského chata hut (Chata kpt. Nálepku), 1462 m. A green-markered trail branches off to the hut. From the fork, we continue our tour for 10 more minutes on the red-markered trail to the panoramic hill, **Lomnická vyhliadka**. The **descent** is made along the same route up to the signpost above the centre waterfall. From here, either hike up to the ground cableway (¼ hr.) or on the yellow-markered path along the Studený potok down to the railway stop of the mountain railway Tatranská Lesná (1½ hrs.).

26 Téryho chata, 2015 m

Through the Malá Studená dolina valley

Hrebienok – poľana Kamzík – Téryho chata – Päť Spišských plies

Location: Starý Smokovec, 1010 m.
Starting point: Hrebienok, 1280 m, the top station of the ground cableway from Starý Smokovec.
Parking: At the church beneath the valley station of the ground cableway.
Walking Times: Hrebienok – Téryho chata 2½ hrs.; descent 2 hrs. Total walking time 4½ hrs.
Grade: Finished pathway, steep at the end. The entire tour is marked.
Highest point: The Téryho chata hut, 2015 m.
Refreshments/Accommodation: The huts Zamkovského chata (Chata kpt. Nálepku) and Téryho chata.

Téryho chata is a hut built of stone and visible from far away that is situated on a high ledge on the fourth terrace step of the Malá Studená dolina valley.

From **Hrebienok**, walk on the red-markered path in a northwesterly direction to the crossing of the hiking paths at the mountain meadow **poľana Kamzík**. Beware of falling rock! Continue along the red-markered pathway to the fork, 1462 m. Go to the left (green markers), past the Zamkovského chata hut (Chata kpt. Nálepku) and uphill into the **Malá Studená dolina** valley.

Behind the third terrace, the pathway leads under the waterfall and to the western side of the valley. The path steeply ascends a scree cone in serpentine curves under the wall of the Prostredný hrot. Behind a narrow opening between boulders, the

The Téryho chata hut and Predné Spišské pleso lake.

path reaches the last slope, which leads to the **hut**.
The **descent** follows the same route.

27 Priečne sedlo, 2352 m

Difficult crossing over a rocky saddle

Hrebienok – Téryho chata – Priečne sedlo – Zbojnícka chata – Hrebienok

Location: Starý Smokovec, 1010 m.
Starting point: Hrebienok, 1280 m, the top station of the ground cableway from Starý Smokovec.
Parking: At the church beneath the valley station of the ground cableway in Starý Smokovec.
Walking Times: Hrebienok – Téryho chata 2½ hrs.; further to Priečne sedlo 1½ hrs.; to Zbojnícka chata 1½ hrs. Back to Hrebienok 2 hrs. Total walking time 7½ hrs.
Grade: A finished pathway in the valley; ascent to the saddle secured with chains, on

the descent, a short section on a detritus-filled slope. The tour is marked, but the crossing is only possible when no snow is present. Due to the popularity of this tour, it is advisable to cross the saddle before 11:00 a.m. It is not permitted to cross the saddle in the opposite direction.
Highest point: The Priečne sedlo saddle, 2352 m.
Refreshments/Accommodation: The huts Zamkovského chata (Chata kpt. Nálepku) and Zbojnícka chata.

Priečne sedlo, a narrow, double gap between the peaks of Široká veža and Priečne veža, offers the only opportunity to cross this mountain crest. Since the scree-filled gully running down from the saddle into Dolinka pod Sedielkom valley is often filled with snow well into the summer and thus not suitable for the ascent, the pathway leads to the right on the rocks, secured with chains. You can avoid possible »traffic jams« on the chains by making your ascent early in the day.

As described in Tour 26, proceed to the **Téryho chata** hut and continue to the northwest on rocky slabs, following the yellow and green markers. Continue

Široká veža, Priečne sedlo and Priečna veža.

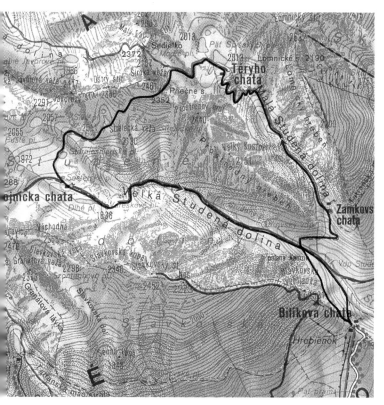

over the outlet of **Veľké Spišské pleso** lake and over the southeast foothill of the Malý Ľadový štít into the **Dolinka pod Sedlielkom** valley to the signpost. Go left (yellow markers) to the rocks at the foot of Široká veža mountain – to the right of the gorge of the Priečne sedlo wind gap. Traverse boulders, secured with chains, to the **wind gap**.

An uncomfortable, short **descent** on a detritus-strewn slope awaits us on the other side. We walk below the southern wall of the mountain Široká veža on a path leading past the Sivé plesá lakes to the **Zbojnícka chata** hut. From there, a blue-markered trail leads downhill to Veľká Studená dolina valley. From the mountain meadow poľana Kamzík, you can take a red-markered path to the ground cableway – to **Starý Smokovec**.

28 Prostredný hrot, 2441 m

A beautiful, but difficult summit to access

Hrebienok – Téryho chata – Sedlo za Prostredným – Prostredný hrot

Location: Starý Smokovec, 1010 m.
Starting point: Hrebienok, 1280 m, top station of the ground cableway from Starý Smokovec.
Parking: At the church beneath the valley station of the ground cableway.
Walking Times: Hrebienok – Téryho chata 2½ hrs.; to the saddle 2 hrs.; to the summit 1 hr.; descent through Veľká Studená dolina valley 4½ hrs. Total walking time 10 hrs.

Grade: Safety rope required! No markers, no chains, exposed location. This tour is only recommended for experienced mountain hikers. Only permitted in the company of a mountain guide!
Highest points: Prostredný hrot, 2441 m, optional: Žltá veža, 2385 m.
Refreshments/Accommodation: The huts Zamkovského chata (Chata kpt. Nálepku), Téryho chata.

The remarkable peak of Prostredný hrot is the highest in the mountain crest between the valleys Malá and Veľká Studená dolina. Its steep escarpments,

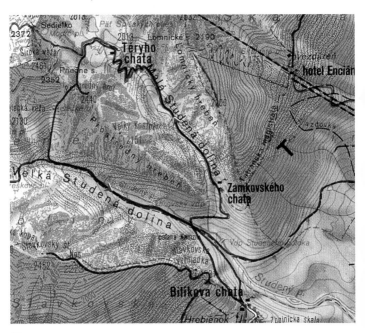

Žltá veža, Malý hrot and Prostredný hrot.

which plunge down on its southeast side, are subject to falling rock. In the north, the peak descends in an attractive face whose divisions enable an ascent route.

As described in Tour 26, go to the **Téryho chata** hut. From there, start on a yellow and green-markered pathway in a northwesterly direction; however, before the first hill, head to the left, over scree, beneath the north face. In this face, you can see a belt of rocks which divides the wall in the middle. Climb up the steep gully and onto the lower left edge of the belt. Once on the belt, go uphill to the right, to the **saddle** between Malý hrot and Žltá veža. The steep upswing of the peak is bypassed on the east side up to the southeast crest, which leads to the **summit**. (From the saddle, 10 min. on Žltá veža; easy). The **descent** is made on the ascent route into the saddle Sedlo za Prostredným. Walk along the gully to the south, and downhill over scree to the blue-markered pathway, which brings us back to the starting point.

29 Ľadový štít, 2627 m

Over the »stone horse« to the third-highest summit in the High Tatra

Hrebienok – Téryho chata – Ľadová priehyba – Ľadový štít

Location: Starý Smokovec, 1010 m.
Starting point: Hrebienok, 1280 m, the top station of the ground cableway from Starý Smokovec.
Parking: At the church beneath the valley station of the ground cableway.
Walking Times: Hrebienok – Téryho chata 2½ hrs.; to the saddle 2 hrs.; to the summit 1 hr.; descent to hut 2 hrs. Total walking time 10 hrs.

Grade: From the Téryho chata hut, partially steep; on the ridge, sections with Difficulty Grade I. Very exposed.
Highest point: The summit Ľadový štít, 2627 m.
Refreshments/Accommodation: The huts Chata kpt. Nálepku-Zamkovského chata and Téryho chata.

The northeastern ridge of the Ľadový štít ends in the rather inconspicuous, small saddle Ľadová priehyba, 2500 m. This saddle is connected to the valley floor via a slanted ramp, on which our ascent leads.
As described in Tour 26, go to the **Téryho chata** hut. Continue to the northwest, initially on a yellow and green-markered pathway, but before the first hill, turn right onto an unmarked pathway. Walk over scree, between the lake on the right and the slope of Malý Ľadový štít on the left, at a moderate incline, to the **end of the valley**. In some sections, the path disappears completely. In the valley end, there are two scree cones, the right one

Ľadová dolinka and the Ľadový štít.

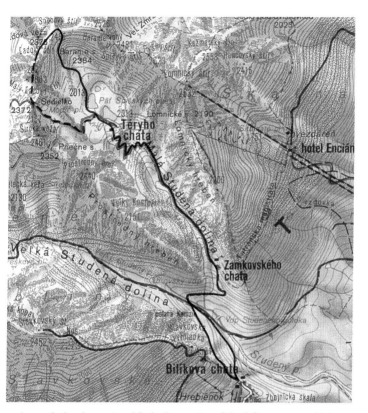

underneath the deepest saddle in the crest, and the left one, over which our ramp starts. On it, we head diagonally uphill to the left onto the crest, which reaches the saddle **Ľadová priehyba**. Continue along the crest in a southwesterly direction. Here, there are a few exposed rocky teeth to traverse. Safety ropes are required! Due to this 20-m long section, the entire route has been named »Over the Stone Horse«. However, there is also another ascent option: From the saddle Ľadová priehyba, go over the belt of rocks straight across the northeastern face to the western ridge, and along it, to the summit. The **descent** is made along the ascent route. Only if conditions are favourable: Bypass the Malý Ľadový štít summit to the Sedielko saddle on belts, and return to the hut along the green-markered trail.

30 Baranie rohy, 2526 m

On the chamois path to the summit in the main crest

Hrebienok – Téryho chata – Baranie sedlo – Baranie rohy

Location: Starý Smokovec, 1010 m.
Starting point: Hrebienok, 1280 m, the top station of the ground cableway from Starý Smokovec.
Parking: At the church beneath the valley station of the ground cableway.
Walking Times: Hrebienok – Téryho chata 2½ hrs.; on to the saddle 1½ hrs.; to the summit ½ hr. Descent along the same route 3½ hrs. Total walking time 8 hrs.
Grade: From the hut, a path which is only partially well-trodden, otherwise scree-covered; from the saddle to the summit, sections with Difficulty Grade I. No markings, no safeguards. Only permitted in the company of a mountain guide!
Highest point: Baranie rohy, 2526 m.
Refreshments/Accommodation: The huts Chata kpt. Nálepku- Zamkovského chata, Téryho chata.

The Baranie rohy is a striking peak with a slanted summit terrace north of the hut Téryho chata. Actually, it has three peaks: the highest is the southeast peak; right behind it is the northwest peak, and about 100 m further on the third, which forms a junction in the main crest and is called Barania strážnica.

As described in Tour 26, go to the **Téryho chata** hut, and from there, head north over the stream. On the other side of the lake, beneath the mountain tower Spišská veža, go to a swell, and over it into the detritus-filled gully, which gets narrower as it ascends, and finally, ends in the saddle **Baranie sedlo**. On the south side of the crest, head to the northwest, to the summit terrace and onto the **southeast summit**.

The **descent** follows the same route.

The peaks of Baranie rohy and Čierny štít.

31 Skalnaté pleso, 1751 m

With the cableway to the mountain lake at the foot of Lomnický štít

Tatranská Lomnica – Skalnaté pleso – Hrebienok – Starý Smokovec

Location: Lomnica, 850 m.
Starting point: The valley station of one of the two cableways to the mountain lake Skalnaté pleso.
Parking: Parking spaces at the valley cableway stations.
Walking times: Ride up with the cableway to Skalnaté pleso lake, 20 min. Ascent to Hrebienok 1½ hrs.; from here, with the ground cableway to Starý Smokovec 10 min. Total

walking time 1½ hrs.
Grade: Finished pathway. The entire tour leads downhill, is marked, and well-travelled.
Highest point: Skalnaté pleso, the top station of the cableway, 1764 m.
Refreshments/Accommodation: The restaurant Encián in the building of the top station of the cableway, the hut Chata kpt. Nálepku- Zamkovského chata.

The mountain lake Skalnaté pleso is a very popular tourist destination in the High Tatra, which is ideal for a half-day excursion.
From the **top station** of the cableway, travel downhill to the south on the red-markered pathway, past the abandoned huts **Skalnatá chata** and, on a moderate descent, straight across the eastern slope of the Lomnický hrebeň

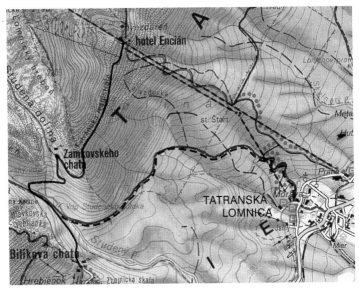

»Lake« Skalnaté pleso, in the background the mountain Malá Svišťovka.

to the panoramic hill **Lomnická vyhliadka**. Here, the path turns to the northwest and arrives at the forest. Not far from the hut Chata kpt. Nálepku-Zamkovského chata, the trail leads in front of the giant waterfall down to the mountain meadow **poľana Kamzík**. Continue either uphill to Hrebienok (red markers) or, from the signposts above the waterfalls, over the bridge under the centre waterfall (blue markers) and to **Tatranská Lomnica** to the valley station of the small cableway; from the bridge, it takes 1½ hrs.

32 Lomnické sedlo, 2190 m, and Lomnický hrebeň, 2211 m

Panoramic walk on a rocky crest

Skalnaté pleso – Lomnické sedlo – Lomnický hrebeň

Location: Tatranská Lomnická, 850 m.
Starting point: Skalnaté pleso, top station of the cableway from Tatranská Lomnická, 1764 m. Parking spaces at the valley station.
Walking times: From the top station at Lake Skalnaté pleso to the chairlift 5 min.; ride with chairlift 20 min.; further on foot 20 min.

Grade: A finished pathway, marked, moderate ascent. Well-frequented tour.
Highest point: Veľká Lomnická veža, 2211 m.
Refreshments/Accommodation: Restaurant Encián in the building of the top station of the cableway.

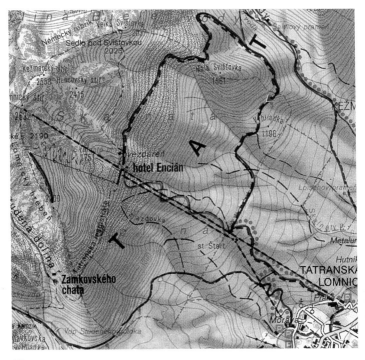

Lomnický hreben and Lomnický štít.

Lomnické sedlo, a flat saddle between the Lomnický hrebeň crest on the left and the Lomnický štít peak on the right, is the starting point for the easiest ascent onto Lomnický štít.

From the **top station** of the cableway at lake Skalnaté pleso, head to the southwest for about 150 m to the chairlift; ride up. From its top station, go uphill to the **saddle** and, following the green-markered pathway, to its **highest point**. From lake Skalnaté pleso, you can return to Tatranská Lomnická on foot: walk along the blue-markered pathway from the observatory over the saddle Sedlo pod Malou Svišťovkou and to the intermediate station Štart; 1½ hrs. From there, either continue with the cableway or along the green-markered pathway in ½ hr. to the valley station in **Tatranská Lomnica**.

33 Lomnický štít, 2632 m

To the second-highest mountain in the High Tatra

Tatranská Lomnica – Skalnaté pleso – Lomnický štít

Location: Tatranská Lomnica, 850 m.
Starting point: Skalnaté pleso, 1764 m, top station of the cableway from Tatranská Lomnica. parking spaces at the valley station of the cableway in Tatranská Lomnica.
Walking times: From Lomnické sedlo to the summit 1½ hrs. Total walking time including return to the valley location 5 – 6 hrs.
Grade: A marked trail to the saddle, further through scree and boulders. Steeper sections of the route are secured with chains and cramps, but not marked. Only permitted in the company of a mountain guide!
Highest point: Lomnický štít, 2632 m.
Refreshments/Accommodation: The restaurant at Skalnaté pleso, buffet at Lomnický štít.

Lomnický štít is, without a doubt, the most significant mountain in the High Tatra, and thanks to the cableway, also the most frequented. Three ridges extend from its peak. Of these, the south ridge is relatively easy to climb. Its eastern flank enables our ascent.

From **Skalnaté pleso**, take the chairlift to under the saddle **Lomnické sedlo**. A short path leads to the saddle, and from there, head up to the right through scree onto the **south ridge**. Continue along the ridge to the Lomnická kopa

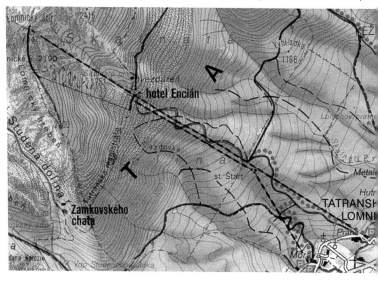

Lomnický štít from the east.

hill, and then, in a somewhat long crossing, to the right (there are chains) to a short wall secured with cramps. Go up through this wall into the summit gorge and, along chains, on to the **summit**. The **descent** follows the same route, or you can take the cableway back to Tatranská Lomnica.

34 Kežmarský štít, 2558 m

On the trail of the first conquerors of the High Tatra

Skalnaté pleso – Cmiter – Huncovské sedlo – Kežmarský štít

Location: Tatranská Lomnica, 850.
Starting point: Skalnaté pleso, the top station of the cableway from Tatranská Lomnica, 1764 m.
Parking: Parking spaces at the valley station of the cableway.
Walking times: Skalnaté pleso – Huncovské sedlo 1¾ hrs.; on to the summit 1¼ hrs.; descent 2½ hrs. Total walking time 5½ hrs.
Grade: The pathway only leads up to the start of the Cmiter basin; continue in a detritus-strewn gully and over scree-covered slopes without markers. In the summit area, difficult orientation. Only permitted in the company of a mountain guide!
Highest points: Malý Kežmarský štít, 2513 m, Kežmarský štít, 2558 m.
Refreshments/Accommodation: Restaurant Encián in the building of the top station of the cableway at Skalnaté pleso lake. No food or accommodation along the route.

From **Skalnaté pleso** lake, go north on the red-markered pathway to the observatory, then uphill to the fork at the vista point Huncovská vyhliadka. Continue to the west on an unmarked path, and from the basin, go right to the

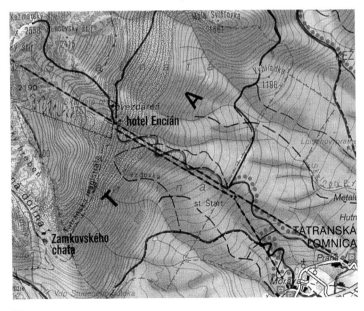

mouth of the largest detritus gully. Climb upward on it; when halfway up, head left to the rib and uphill to the **saddle**. Continue on the northeastern side of the crest in the gap between Malý Kežmarský štít on the right and Kežmarský štít on the left. **Both summits** are accessible without difficulty. If the terrain on the northeastern side of the crest over Huncovské sedlo is snowy or icy, you can, as a consolation, climb up from the saddle to the nearby mountain Huncovský štít. The **descent** from Kežmarský štít is made along the same route; from Huncovský štít, you can also climb down on the moderately-inclined southwest slope on the pathway to the vista point Huncovská vyhliadka.

The Kežmarský štít summit, as seen from Skalnaté pleso lake.

35 Veľká Svišťovka, 2037 m

A non-strenuous route downhill to Zelené pleso lake

Skalnaté pleso – Huncovská vyhliadka – Veľká Svišťovka – Zelené pleso – Tatranská Lomnica

Location: Tatranská Lomnica, 850 m.
Starting point: Skalnaté pleso, the top station of the cableway from Tatranská Lomnica, 1764 m.
Parking: The parking spaces at the valley stations of the cableways in Tatranská Lomnica.
Walking times: Skalnaté pleso – Veľká Svišťovka 1 hr.; Zelené pleso 1 hr.; Tatranská

Lomnica 3 hrs. Total walking time 5 hrs.
Grade: Finished pathway. From the hut on, forest trail. The entire hike is marked. Only two short ascents, otherwise downhill.
Highest point: Veľká Svišťovka, 2037 m.
Refreshments/Accommodation: The hut Chata pri Zelenom plese, formerly called Brnčalova chata.

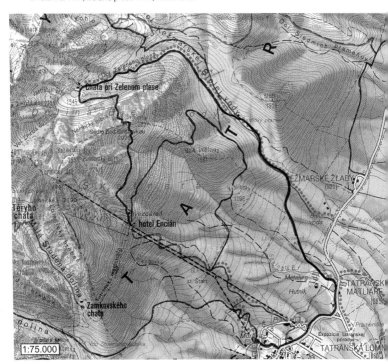

1:75.000

94

The Veľká Svišťovka peak, to the left the saddle Sedlo pod Svišťovkou.

The summit of Veľká Svišťovka has been visited for ages by treasure-hunters. An old mine can also be seen on our tour.

From **Skalnaté pleso** lake, walk along the red-markered pathway to the north, past the observatory, and uphill to the fork at the vista point **Huncovská vyhliadka**, 1877 m. From here, head straight across the eastern slope of the mountain Huncovský štít, and finally, to the saddle **Sedlo pod Svišťovkou**. Head to the right onto the **summit**.

Take the same route back. From the saddle, head downhill over the northern slope and around 22 serpentine curves on a grassy ridge, carefully over the mouth of the gully that plunges down from our saddle. Continue in a long crossing at the foot of the wall, continually moderately downhill, to **Čierne pleso** lake, and beyond it, to the hut **Chata pri Zelenom plese**, formerly called Brnčalova chata.

Returning to Tatranská Lomnica: walk along the yellow-markered pathway to the signpost above the Biela voda stream, 1977 m, and further along the blue-markered pathway through the forest to Tatranské Matliare and, next to the main road, on an unmarked path to Tatranská Lomnica. This tour can also be done in the opposite direction; however, in doing so, an ascent of 1200 m must be surmounted.

36 Zelené pleso, 1545 m, and Veľké Biele pleso, 1612 m

A picturesque valley basin at the foot of the highest face of the High Tatra

Biela voda – Zelené pleso – Veľké Biele pleso – Biela voda

Location: Tatranská Lomnica, 850 m.
Starting point: The bus stop Biela voda, 925 m; Located 4 km to the northeast of Tatranská Lomnica.
Parking: The car park in Tatranská Lomnica at the museum near the bus stop.
Walking times: Biela voda – Zelené pleso 3 hrs.; further on to Biele pleso ½ hr; descent to Biela voda 2½ hrs. or to Tatranská Lomnica

3 hrs. Total walking time 6–7 hrs.
Grade: Up to Zelené pleso lake a forest path, continuing on a marked pathway. Moderate gradient; the entire tour is marked.
Highest point: Biele pleso, 1612 m.
Refreshments/Accommodation: The hut Chata pri Zelenom plese, formerly called Brnčalova chata.

Zelené pleso is one of the five green lakes in the High Tatra. It is situated on the valley floor of the romantic mountain basin at the foot of four sloped valleys. South of the lake, the highest face of the High Tatra juts into the sky: the 900-m high north face of the Malý Kežmarský štít.

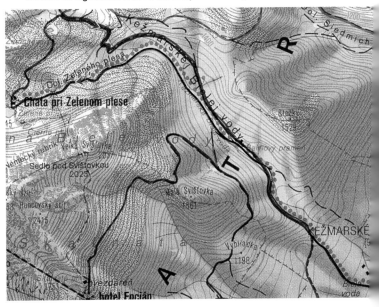

The Malý Kežmarský štít above the basin of Zelené pleso lake.

From the **Biela voda** bus stop, walk along an access road (yellow markers) to the fork above the Šalviový prameň spring, 1200 m. Head toward the left over the bridge, along the right bank of the Zelený potok stream to the hut **Chata pri Zelenom plese**. Continue on the path to the northeast (red markers) to **Veľké Biele pleso** lake.

The **descent** to the southeast: follow the blue-markered path to the Šalviový prameň spring and to the bus stop Biela voda; or, from the signpost above the Biela voda stream, 1077 m, walk along the blue-markered pathway over Tatranské Matliare, and finally next to the street on the unmarked path to Tatranská Lomnica.

37 Jahňací štít, 2229 m

Underway in the eastern part of the High Tatra

Zelené pleso – Červená dolina – Kolové sedlo – Jahňací štít

Location: Tatranská Lomnica, 850 m.
Starting point: The hut Chata pri Zelenom plese, 1551 m. Accessible from Tatranská Lomnica as described in Tour 36 in 3½ hrs. or from the bus stop Biela voda in 3 hrs.
Parking: The car park at the museum in Tatranská Lomnica.
Walking times: Zelené pleso – Červená dolina ¾ hrs.; Kolové sedlo 1¼ hrs.; Jahňací

štít ½ hr.; descent to hut 1½ hrs. Total walking time 10 hrs.
Grade: This is a non-maintained but marked pathway that is mostly steep and secured with chains in the difficult section under the ridge.
Highest point: Jahňací štít, 2229 m.
Refreshments/Accommodation: The hut Chata pri Zelenom plese.

Jahňací štít is the hub of four mountain crests, and at the same time, is the last peak in the eastern part of the High Tatra. Its summit offers an extraordinarily extensive panorama.

Starting at the signpost at the **hut**, follow the yellow-markered path over the steps upward into **Červená dolina** valley, and, along a rather long ascent, into the valley end. Here, beneath the mountain crest, walk to the right into the cleft (chains), and over it to the Kolové sedlo wind gap. The ascent continues on the west side of the ridge. Up further, the path leads over a striking rocky rib to the northwest side crest. From there, the path, steadily ascending, comes back around toward our southern crest repeatedly, which it reaches in a scree-covered saddle right under the **summit**.

The return is made along the same route. Pay attention to find the correct crossover spot into the Červená dolina valley! Following this path to the south will get you lost!

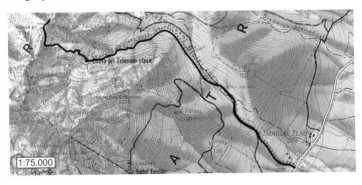

Jahňací štít, as seen from Červená dolina valley.

38 Jastrabia veža, 2137 m

A rock tower steeped in legend above Zelené pleso lake

Zelené pleso – Červená dolina – Jastrabie sedlo – Jastrabia veža

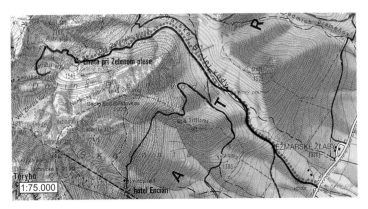

Location: Tatranská Lomnica, 850 m.
Starting point: The hut Chata pri Zelenom plese, 1551 m. Accessible from Tatranská Lomnica, as described in Tour 36, in 3½ hrs.; from the bus stop Biela voda in 3 hrs.
Parking: The car park next to the museum in Tatranská Lomnica.
Walking times: Zelené pleso – Červená dolina ¾ hr.; on to Jastrabie sedlo ¾ hr.; to Jastrabia veža 1 hr.; descent to the hut

1½ hrs. Total walking time 10 hrs.
Grade: From Červená dolina valley to the Jastrabie sedlo saddle, a non-maintained, unmarked path. Further, an exposed rocky ridge for which a safety rope is necessary. Only permitted in the company of a mountain guide!
Highest point: Jastrabia veža, 2137 m.
Refreshments/Accommodation: The hut Chata pri Zelenom plese.

The Jastrabia veža is the closest peak in the amphitheatre of the mountains surrounding Lake Zelené pleso. When looking out from the hut, its sheer walls and apparent inaccessibility make it conspicuous. The old Spiš designation of the mountain as a »Jewel Tower« goes back to the legend that there used to be a jewel on the summit. During the summer nights, one could supposedly see its illuminated red glow from far away. Once, a young shepherd boy succeeded in climbing to the summit, but at the moment that he wanted to touch the jewel, the spirit of the Tatra cut him down with a thunderbolt, and the jewel fell into Červená dolina valley and disappeared in the spot where Červená pleso lake (Red Lake) is located today.

Starting from the sign at the **hut**, follow the yellow-markered path up the steep steps into the **Červená dolina** valley to the hill above Červená pleso lake. Here, a poorly visible, unmarked path branches off to the left at an elevation of 1883 m. Follow it to the saddle **Jastrabie sedlo**, and further to the left on rocky slabs under the overhanging rocks. Walking under them, cross to the right. Beyond a corner, the route returns to the ridge and follows it to the **summit**. There is also an easier alternative: Walk beneath the saddle, on the side of the Červená dolina valley on a rocky belt straight through the northern wall to behind the summit, and on the eastern slope, to the highest point. There are two belts here; normally, hikers walk along the upper one, which also serves as the **descent** route from the summit.

Jastrabia veža, as seen from the hut Chata pri Zelenom plese.

39 Poľana pod Muráňom, 1100 m

Through the idyllic promontory of Belianske Tatry

Tatranská Javorina – Poľana pod Muráňom – Dolina Bieleho potoka – Hunting Lodge – Tatranská Javorina

Location: Tatranská Javorina, 1000 m.
Starting point: Signpost in the street curve at the southwest edge of town.
Parking: Car park in the centre of town, parking spaces at Hotel Poľana.
Walking times: Tatranská Javorina – mountain meadow Poľana pod Muráňom 40 min.; from there, descent to church ½ hr.; further to panoramic hill near the hunting lodge and return to the town ½ hr. Total walking time 2 hrs.
Grade: An access road up to the mountain meadow Poľana pod Muráňom; from the church to the hunting lodge, a road with a slight gradient.
Highest point: Poľana pod Muráňom, 1100 m.
Refreshments/Accommodation: The guesthouse in Tatranská Javorina and the Hotel Poľana are inviting for a rest.

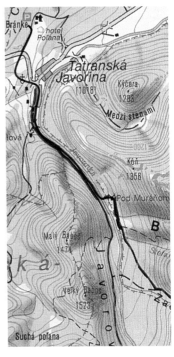

From the meadow Poľana pod Muráňom, you have a beautiful view of the northern side of the main crest of the High Tatra – from the peak of Kolový štít, to the peak of Baranie rohy and Ľadový štít, to the peaks of Javorové štíty.
From the signpost at the southwest edge of town, follow an access road (blue and green markers) to the south to the sign above the **waterworks**. Turn left and head over the bridge to the **mountain meadow** Poľana pod Muráňom. The **return route** follows the same route. From the signpost in town, head west to the church, and now, either onto the meadow or to the road and on to Hotel Poľana. The hunting lodge is situated directly behind the hotel.

Tatranská Javorina with the peaks of Kolový štít, Baranie rohy and Ľadový štít.

40 Kopské sedlo, 1749 m

To the saddle between Vysoké Tatry and Belianske Tatry

Tatranská Javorina – Kopské sedlo – Veľké Biele pleso – Tatranská Kotlina

Location: Tatranská Javorina, 1000 m.
Starting point: The signpost in Tatranská Javorina on the southwest edge of town.
Parking: Car park in the centre of town.

Walking times: Tatranská Javorina – Kopské sedlo 3 hrs.; to Tatranská Kotlina 3 hrs. Total walking time 6 hrs.
Grade: Forest trails, maintained pathways without significant gradient; marked.
Highest point: Kopské sedlo, 1749 m, Predné Kopské sedlo, 1778 m.
Refreshments/Accommodation: Open shelter in Borček, the hut Plesnivec. Both only offer shelter from the rain.

From the signpost in **Tatranská Javorina**, walk along an access road in a southerly direction (blue and green markers) for 2.2 km to the bridge above the waterworks. Go over the bridge to the left (blue markers), beneath the **caretaker's house** and into Zadné Meďodoly valley. The forest trail leads through that part of the area called Borček (shel-

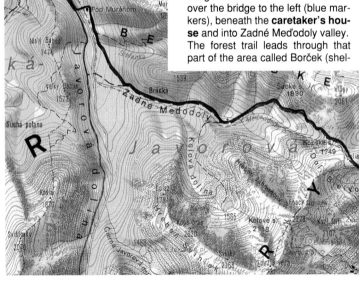

The Kopské sedlo saddle, in the foreground Veľké Biele pleso lake.

ter), and over a short, rocky narrow pass, called Bránka. Follow along the stream to the spring Skorušia studnicka, 1375 m. Continue on the path in open terrain over both **saddles** Kopské sedlá to **Veľké Biele pleso** lake. The continuation of the tour follows along a green-markered pathway to the **Plesnivec hut** and to **Tatranská Kotlina** to the bus stop. From Veľké Biele pleso, you can also walk down to Tatranské Matliare along the blue-markered pathway.

41 Sedielko, 2372 m

Over the main crest on the south side of the High Tatra

Tatranská Javorina – Javorová dolina – Sedielko – Starý Smokovec

Location: Tatranská Javorina, 1000 m.
Starting point: The signpost in Tatranská Javorina on the southwest edge of town.
Parking: Car park in the centre of town.
Walking times: Tatranská Javorina – Sedielko 5 hrs.; Starý Smokovec 3½ hrs. Total walking time 8½ hrs.
Grade: At the beginning, an access road, later a forest trail, further up, a narrow pathway. The

descent from the saddle is done over a scree-covered slope in some spots, the last part on a developed pathway. The entire tour is marked. Only accessible if there is no snow on the slopes of the saddle Sedielko.
Highest point: Sedielko, 2372 m.
Refreshments/Accommodation: The huts Téryho chata, Chata kpt. Nálepku-Zamkovského chata.

Sedielko is a wide saddle in the main crest of the High Tatra between the peaks of Ľadový štít and Široká veža. It leans into Javorová dolina valley with a sparsely grassy slope – over the serpentine curves of our pathway; to southwest, in Malá Studená dolina valley, it falls with a steeper, scree-co-

The end of Malá Studená dolina, to the right, Sedielko saddle.

106

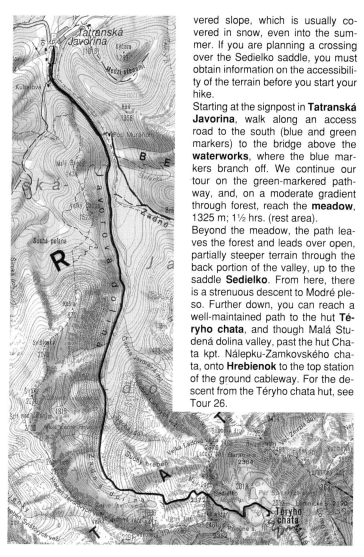

vered slope, which is usually covered in snow, even into the summer. If you are planning a crossing over the Sedielko saddle, you must obtain information on the accessibility of the terrain before you start your hike.

Starting at the signpost in **Tatranská Javorina**, walk along an access road to the south (blue and green markers) to the bridge above the **waterworks**, where the blue markers branch off. We continue our tour on the green-markered pathway, and, on a moderate gradient through forest, reach the **meadow**, 1325 m; 1½ hrs. (rest area).

Beyond the meadow, the path leaves the forest and leads over open, partially steeper terrain through the back portion of the valley, up to the saddle **Sedielko**. From here, there is a strenuous descent to Modré pleso. Further down, you can reach a well-maintained path to the hut **Téryho chata**, and though Malá Studená dolina valley, past the hut Chata kpt. Nálepku-Zamkovského chata, onto **Hrebienok** to the top station of the ground cableway. For the descent from the Téryho chata hut, see Tour 26.

42 Bielovodská dolina

Through the most beautiful valley of the High Tatra

Lysá poľana – Žabia poľana – Litvorové pleso – Poľský hrebeň – Starý Smokovec

Location: Lysá poľana, 970 m.
Starting point: The signpost at the border bridge over which the street leads into Poland.
Parking: The car park in Lysá poľana.
Walking times: Lysá poľana – Poľana pod Vysokou 2½ hrs.; to Litvorové pleso lake 1½ hrs.; Poľský hrebeň 1½ hrs.; descent to mountain hotel Sliezsky dom 1½ hr.; from there to Starý Smokovec 2 hrs. Total walking time 9 hrs.
Grade: At the beginning, a comfortable access road with a moderate gradient

(pleasant walk), at higher elevations a narrow path only partly maintained. For the descent, the path is secured with chains. A long, strenuous tour.
Highest point: The saddle Poľský hrebeň, 2200 m.
Refreshments/Accommodation: Two small overhead shelters in Bielovodská dolina valley offer only protection from the rain. You can stop at the mountain hotel Sliezsky dom in Velická dolina valley.

Bielovodská dolina valley with the peaks Mlynár, Vysoká, Rysy and Malý Žabý štít.

Bielovodská dolina is a 10-km long valley, which moderately ascends from Lysá poľana along the border river Biela voda to the mountain meadow Poľana pod Vysokou. In the lower port, there is an old caretaker's house on a large meadow, offering a unique view of the surrounding mountain crests. Up to this point, you can also take a comfortable walk.

From the **bridge** on the border in Lysá poľana, go to the left (blue markers). On the access road beneath Tisovky rock (overhead shelter), we traverse the meadow containing the **caretaker's house**, and further up, cross the river. We continue along its southwest bank to the mountain meadow **Žabia poľana**, 1146 m (overhead shelter). From the meadow, head over the bridge to the east side of the small river, and continue to the mountain meadow Poľana pod Vysokou, 1315 m.

Follow the path further up, in serpentine curves. To the right, you can see the waterfall Hviezdoslavov vodopád. The fork, 1605 m, is located over the first valley step, in Kačacia dolina. Here, go left, up a continually steep gradient, to the east to **Litvorové pleso** lake, and, in the same direction, on to the hollow between Hrubá veža (to the left) and Velický štít (to the right). Above Zamrznuté pleso lake, 2047 m, walk to the sign beneath the saddle Poľský hrebeň and, finally, to the right (green markers) steeply up to the saddle **Poľský hrebeň**.

Descent into Velická dolina valley: see Tour 23.

1:75.000

43 Ždiar – Belianska jaskyňa

A visit to a Goral community

Ždiar – Monkova dolina – Strednica – Ždiar – Belianska jaskyňa

Location: Ždiar, 895 m.
Starting point: Bus stop Ždiar »Tatra«, near the centre of town on the main road.
Parking: On the green-markered access road near the bus stop.
Walking times: Ždiar – Monkova dolina ½ hr.; on to Strednica ¾ hrs.; descent ¾ hrs.; Tatranská Kotlina – Belianska jaskyňa 20 min.; visit to the limestone cave 1¼ hr.;

descent ¼ hr. Total walking time 5 hrs.
Grade: Most of the tour consists of pleasant forest trails; a steeper path only leads along Strednica hill.
Highest points: Strednica hill, 1020 m, the limestone cave Belianska jaskyňa, 885 m.
Refreshments/Accommodation: The restaurant in Ždiar.

This tour leads us into the surroundings of Ždiar and to the limestone cave Belianska jaskyňa, which is open to the public along a length of over 1 km . In the cave, there are beautiful stalactite and stalagmite adornments, a few large rooms, and small lakes. It was discovered by treasure-hunters in the 18th century.

From the bus stop »Tatra« in Ždiar, we leave the town in a southwesterly direction on a side access road (green markers). At the end of the access road, a pathway leads through the forest and to the ski meadow on **Strednica** hill. We walk along the main road to the north, and down along the side road.

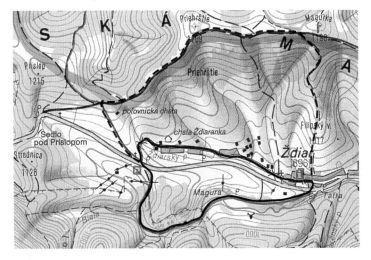

The village of Ždiar with the two highest peaks of the Balea Tatra.

You can then return to the starting point through Ždiar. If you also wish to visit the **limestone caves**, drive or take the bus to **Tatranská Kotlina** and get off at the bus stop »Cave« = jaskyňa; there is also a car park here. From here, walk up to the cave, which is worth seeing, on a forest path (yellow markers). If you do not wish to visit the cave, there is also another hiking option: from Strednica along a path to the northwest, continuing on the mountain slope of Spišská Magura to the northeast (blue markers) and, beneath Margurka, descending to Ždiar (red markers); a total of 2 hours more.

44 Morskie Oko, 1393 m

An unexpectedly beautiful mountain lake under the rocky Mnich (monk)

Włosienica – Morskie Oko – Czarny Staw

Morskie Oko.

Location: Łysa Polana, 970 m.
Starting point: Włosienica, 1310 m. Overhead shelter, buffet. Accessible from the car park Palenica Białczańska in 45 min., with several Goral carriages that run in the summer for visitors. Distance 7 km .
Parking: Palenica Białczańska, 980 m, parking attendant. From the location of Łysa Polana, 1 km to the southwest.
Walking times: Włosienica – Morskie Oko 20 min.; walk around the lake 45 min.; side-

trip to Czarny Staw 1¼ hrs. Total walking time 2½ – 3 hrs.
Grade: In the beginning, a road which is closed to public traffic. A maintained pathway leads around the mountain lake Morskie Oko. The tour is marked and well-visited.
Highest point: Morskie Oko, 1393 m; Czarny Staw, 1583 m.
Refreshments/Accommodation: The hut Schronisko przy Morskim Oku, 1404 m, with restaurant and overnight accommodation.

Morskie Oko, a mountain lake in a picturesque environment under the northern slopes of the border crest between Poland and Slovakia, with its area of 35 hectares, depth of 51 m, and length of 800 m, is the largest lake in the High Tatra. On its northern shore, the hut Schronisko przy Morskim Oku can be found. From there, looking to the southwest, you can see the steep tower of Mnich (monk), and to the left of it, the three mountains Mengusovské štíty, and to the far left, Rysy.

From Włosienica, walk along the road to the northern shore of **Morskie Oko**, and further to the left, along the 2.5-km long pathway around the lake. When you are halfway around, you can follow the red markers on a 40-minute walk

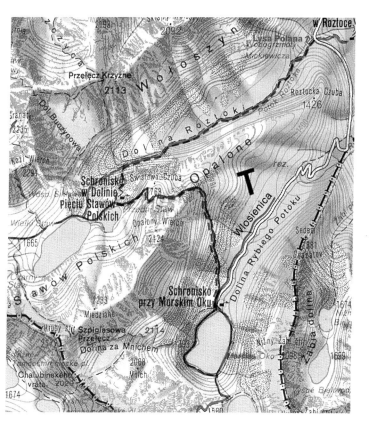

to **Czarny Staw** lake, located up higher. This pathway leads to Rysy, but is much more difficult than the ascent from the south side (Tour 11). If you do not wish to return from Morskie Oko along the same route, or if you do not wish to walk around the lake, you can follow a blue-markered pathway from the hut to the north up to Kepa mountain, 1683 m – a beautiful view of the entire mountain basin including Morskie Oko – and further over the mountain Świstowa Czuba, 1763 m, in 1½ hrs. to the hut Schronisko w Dolinie Pięciu Stawów Polskich. From there, head downhill, first following the black, then the green markers, through Dolina Roztoki valley, and ultimately back via the road to the car park Palenica Białczańska (2 hrs.).

45 Szpiglasowa Przełęcz, 2114 m, and Hrubý štít, 2172 m

On the best pathway of the Polish Tatra to the Border Crest

Włosienica – Morskie Oko – Szpiglasowa Przełęcz – Hrubý štít

Location: Łysa Polana, 970 m.
Starting point: Włosienica, 1310 m; see Tour 44.
Parking: Palenica Białczańska, 980 m, parking attendant. From the location of Łysa Polana, 1 km to the southwest.
Walking times: Włosienica – Szpiglasowa Przełęcz saddle 2¾ hrs.; to the summit of Hrubý štít 10 min. Descent along the same route, 2 hrs. Total walking time 5 hrs.

Grade: From Morskie Oko lake to the Szpiglasowa Przełęcz saddle, a well-built pathway; on to the summit, a maintained trail. The tour is only marked up to the saddle.
Highest point: The summit of Hrubý štít, 2172 m.
Refreshments/Accommodation: See Tour 44.

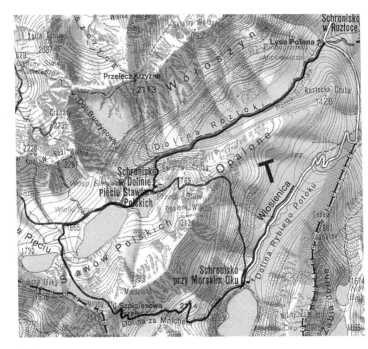

Szpiglasowa Przełęcz and Hrubý štít.

The mountain Hrubý štít forms a junction with the border saddle: from its peak, the secondary ridge bends down to the Miedziane, on which the saddle Szpiglasowa Przełęcz is located, an important crossing between two valleys. While the southeast slope under the saddle offers a pleasant ascent, the northwest slope is steep, and the trail secured with chains.

From **Włosienica**, start on the road, heading in the direction of Morskie Oko, and on the moraine wall – before reaching the hut – go right onto the yellow-markered pathway, which leads in a steady, gentle incline to the small valley between the rocky tower Mnich and our saddle. The route leads up along three long hairpin turns to the saddle **Szpiglasowa Przełęcz**. On the other side, the mountains Svinica (Tour 50) and Kozi Wierch (Tour 46) can be seen. From the saddle, go to the left and over a short slope to the **summit**.

The **descent** follows along the same route. From the saddle, you can also continue the tour and return via the valley Dolina Pięciu Stawów Polskich and Roztoka to the road, which, however, is considerably more difficult and takes about 2 hrs. longer.

46 Kozi Wierch, 2291 m

To the highest mountain in Poland

Wodogrzmoty Mickiewicza – Wielki Staw – Kozi Wierch

Location: Łysa Polana, 970 m.
Starting point: Wodogrzmoty Mickiewicza, 1100 m, accessible from the car park Palenica Białczańska with a Goral carriage in 25 min., or on foot along the road in the direction of Morskie Oko, 3 km .
Parking: Palenica Białczańska, 980 m, parking attendant. From the location Łysa Polana, 1 km to the southwest.
Walking times: Wodogrzmoty Mickiewicza – Wielki Staw 2 hrs.; to the summit 2 hrs.;

descent 3 hrs. Total walking time 7 hrs.
Grade: Through Dolina Roztoki valley, a badly-maintained forest trail, further up a path to the summit. The tour is marked.
Highest point: Kozi Wierch, 2291 m.
Refreshments/Accommodation: Schronisko w Roztoce hut, 1031 m, accessible beneath the Wodogrzmoty Mickiewicza waterfalls in 10 min. On the descent, the hut Schronisko w Delinie Pięciu Stawów Polskich, 1672 m.

Kozi Wierch rises with steep faces above two valleys – only to the southeast does it descend with an accessible slope, along which our ascent leads. The famed »Orla Perl« route runs along the western and eastern ridge, which – although marked – is incomparably more difficult.

From the signpost near the **Wodogrzmoty Mickiewicza** waterfalls, walk to the southwest on a green-markered trail along the Roztoka stream until you arrive under the lake wall through which the 70-meter waterfall Siklawa plunges. Soon after, on a steeper path, we arrive at the northern shore of

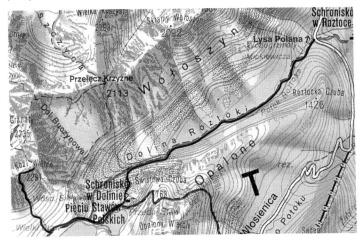

Kozi Wierch from the southeast with the ascent path.

Wlelkl Staw lake. Continue on the blue-markered path (with the option of a side-trip to the left, to the **hut** in 10 min.) to the right over a grassy mountain slope to the second turn-off, where the black-markered path up to the summit begins. We walk to the right, and along the gully descending from the summit, steeply upward in several hairpin turns. Near the ridge, we walk to the right, straight across the upper part of the gully, and following the red-markered path, to the **summit**. The **descent** follows the same route. After a rest at the hut, follow the black-markered path downhill into the valley Dolina Roztoki.

47 Hala Gąsienicowa, 1500 m

To the flower-rich mountain pasture near Zakopane

Kuźnice – Boczań – Przełęcz między Kopami – Schronisko Murowaniec

Location: Zakopane, 900 m.
Starting point: Kuźnice, 1000 m. From the car park in Zakopane, 2 km to the south. Bus connection.
Parking: On the upper, southeastern edge of Zakopane, at the »Rondo« crossing; parking attendant.
Walking times: Kuźnice – Przełęcz między Kopami saddle 1½ hrs.; Schronisko Murowa-

niec ½ hr.; descent through the valley Dolina Jaworzynka 1½ hrs. Total walking time 3½ hrs.
Grade: At the beginning, a forest trail, then a good pathway. The entire tour is marked.
Highest point: Królowa Rowień, 1560 m.
Refreshments/Accommodation: Schronisko Murowaniec, 1500 m, with restaurant and overnight accommodation.

The Hala Gąsienicowa is a wide, flat valley over the wooded foothills southeast of Zakopane. There used to be extensive meadows here, which have recently been increasingly supplanted by mountain pines. Further up, this valley divides into two secondary valleys, in which there are 18 lakes. The hut Schronisko Murowaniec, which is situated in the lower part of the valley, is an important starting point for over ten summit tours in this area.

From Kuźnice, walk to the east over the stream Bystra on the green and blue-markered trail through the pine wood. After about 10 minutes, a green-markered pathway branches off to the left, to Nosal mountain. Following the blue markers, we ascend to the Boczań slope, 1208 m, and further – already

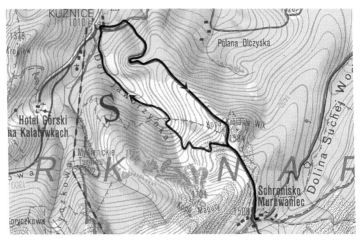

in open terrain – over the Skupniów Uplaz ridge to the saddle **Przełęcz między Kopami**, and thereafter, over the Królowa Rowien elevation to the hut **Schronisko Murowaniec**.

The descent follows the same route up to the saddle, and further along a yellow-markered pathway downhill into the valley of Dolina Jaworzynka, whose exit is situated directly over Kuźnice. If you have enough time, you can extend the tour: on a black-markered path to Zielony Staw lake (good resting places), ½ hr., or on a yellow-markered path up to Kasprov vrch (Kasprowy Wierch) in 1½ hrs, and back with the cableway to Kuźnice.

Hala Gąsienicowa with Zielony Staw and Kasprov vrch (Kasprowy Wierch).

48 Granaty, 2240 m

Ridge hike on the famous »Orla Perc« path

Schronisko Murowaniec – Skrajny Granat – Zadni Granat – Murowaniec

Location: Zakopane, 900 m.
Starting point: Schronisko Murowaniec hut, 1500 m, accessible from Kuźnice (from the car park in Zakopane 2 km to the south; bus connection) in 2 hrs.
Parking: On the upper, southeastern edge of Zakopane, at the »Rondo« crossing; parking attendant.
Walking times: Schronisko Murowaniec hut – Czarny Staw ½ hr.; Czarny Staw – Skrajny Granat 2 hrs.; Skrajny Granat – Zadni Granat ½ hr. Total walking time 5 hrs., including travel to and from Kuznice 8½ hrs.
Grade: A maintained pathway leads to the foot of the wall. The ascent to the first summit is steep and rocky, a difficult spot is secured with cramps. Ridge hike and descent easy. The entire tour is marked.
Highest point: Skrajny Granat, 2225 m; Pośredni Granat, 2234 m; Zadni Granat, 2240 m.
Refreshments/Accommodation: None along the route.

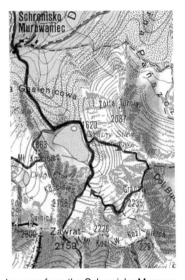

The Granaty, with its three peaks, can be seen from the Schronisko Murowaniec hut, on the left side of the surrounding southern peaks. The famous and most difficult hiking tour of the Tatra, the »Orla Perc« (Eagle Path), leads from Svinica to the saddle Przełęcz Kryżne. The easiest section on the ridge of the three Granat peaks is ideal for our tour.

From the **Schronisko Murowaniec** hut, travel about 100 metres to the southwest, to the sign, and to the left (blue markers) to the northern shore of the lake **Czarny Staw Gąsienicowy**. From there, turn left, along the lake, and after 800 metres, turn left again and follow the yellow-markered pathway diagonally up to the mouth of a prominent detritus-filled gully (see photo). We follow the gully to the right to the rocks on the western rib of the Skrajny Granat. Over rocky slabs (key spot), we access the ridge of the western rib and along it, we walk along short hairpin turns to the summit of **Skrajny Granat**. Continuing to the south (red markers), no longer with difficulty, we traverse the centre peak to the highest, the **Zadni Granat**. The **descent**

The three Granaty peaks, seen from the west.

initially follows the previous direction, but after 200 metres, we turn off down to the left (green markers) on the southwest slope, and subsequently, follow the yellow and finally the blue-markered path to the starting point.

49 Kościelec, 2155 m

A bold peak for discriminating high-altitude tourists

Schronisko Murowaniec – Czarny Staw Gąsienicowy – Przełęcz Karb – Kościelec – Schronisko Murowaniec

Location: Zakopane, 900 m.
Starting point: The Schronisko Murowaniec hut, 1500 m, accessible from Kuźnice (from the car park in Zakopane 2 km to the south; bus connection) in 2 hrs.
Parking: On the upper, southeastern edge of Zakopane, at the »Rondo« crossing.
Walking times: Murowaniec – Czarny Staw Gąsienicowy ½ hr.; Czarny Staw Gąsienicowy – Przełęcz Karb ¾ hr.; Przełęcz Karb – Kościelec 1 hr.; descent 1¾ hrs. Total walking

time 4 hrs., including travel to and from Kuźnice 7½ hrs.
Grade: To Przełęcz Karb, a maintained pathway, ascent to the summit partially rocky, with two climbing spots having Difficulty Grade I, which, however, can be surmounted without ropes. The tour is marked.
Highest point: The saddle Przełęcz Karb, 1853 m; Kościelec, 2155 m.
Refreshments/Accommodation: None along the route.

Kościelec, a steep rocky pyramid, is the most prominent peak in the southern panorama above our starting point. Its northern ridge separates Dolina Gąsienicowa valley into two tributary valleys: our ascent leads through the eastern valley, and the descent through the western valley.

From the hut **Schronisko Murowaniec**, travel about 100 metres to the southwest, to the signpost, and then to the left (blue markers), to the northern shore of **Czarny Staw Gąsienicowy** lake. Here, go to the right (green

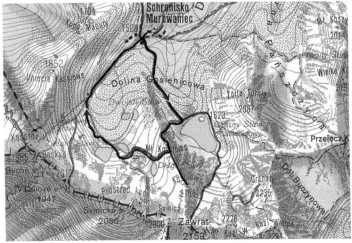

Kościelec from the west.

marker), steeply up to the Maly Kościelec ridge, and along it, walking slightly downhill, to the saddle **Przełęcz Karb**. Over the saddle, the northern ridge expands to a wide slab slope with two somewhat steep cross steps. The first step is the most difficult spot of the tour. From the saddle, following the black markers, you should try and primarily stay closer to the left edge of the slope. From the **summit**, the **descent** follows the same route to the saddle Przełęcz Karb. Further to the left, and in a westerly direction, head downhill on a blue-markered path between several lakes; from Zielony Staw, walk along the black-markered pathway to the starting point.

50 Svinica, 2301 m

Over the Tatra main crest to the Polish fashion mountain

Kasprov vrch – Suché sedlo – Svinické sedlo – Svinica

The Svinica peak from the east. The Zawrat saddle (right) and Hladké sedlo (left).

Location: Zakopane, 900 m.
Starting point: Kuźnice, 1000 m, valley station of the cableway to Kasprov vrch (Polish: Kasprowy Wierch). From the car park in Zakopane, 2 km to the south. Bus connection.
Parking: On the upper, southeastern edge of Zakopane, at the »Rondo« crossing; parking attendant.
Walking times: Ride on the cableway 20 min.; further over the ridge to the saddle 1 hr.; Ascent to summit of Svinica 1 hr.;

descent to the hut Schronisko Murowaniec 2 hrs, to Kuźnice another 1½ hrs. Total walking time 6 hrs.
Grade: From the top station, a pathway to the last saddle, ascent to the Svinica summit rocky, a difficult spot secured with iron cramps. The entire tour is marked.
Highest point: Kasprov vrch, 1985 m; Svinické sedlo, 2050 m; Svinica, 2301 m.
Refreshments/Accommodation: Cableway top station, along descent, Schronisko Murowaniec.

Svinica is a mighty, rocky mountain, and the first from the west in the main crest of the High Tatra.

From the top station of the cableway, walk to the south for about 150 metres to the main crest, which reaches our pathway in the saddle **Suché sedlo** (= Sucha Przełęcz). If, instead of undertaking this tour, you prefer to simply take a walk, you can comfortably walk down to the Schronisko Murowaniec hut in 1 hour (yellow markers). Our tour leads further to the southeast, following the main crest and the red markers, continuously along the national borderline, partly in Polish territory, partly in Slovakian, over **Beskyd** mountain, 2012 m, the saddle **Ľaliové sedlo**, 1947 m, and two rocky hilltops, to the Svinické sedlo saddle (= Swinicowa Przełęcz). Continue beyond the saddle, uphill in the same direction. Further up, the path branches off to the right; to the south, you can circumvent the lower northwest summit, traverse a rocky gully, and climb down an airy bank (there are cramps). Further up, walk through the wind gap of a gully, called »Wrótka« (= little door), on the side of the valley Dolina Pięciu Stawów Polskich. Head downhill on a rocky slope and, following the pathway coming up from the east, from Zawrat, walk diagonally to the left to the **main summit**. The **descent** follows the same route up to the saddle Svinické sedlo. From there, travel to the north on the black-markered path to the hut Schronisko Murowaniec. To continue to Kuźnice, see Tour 47.

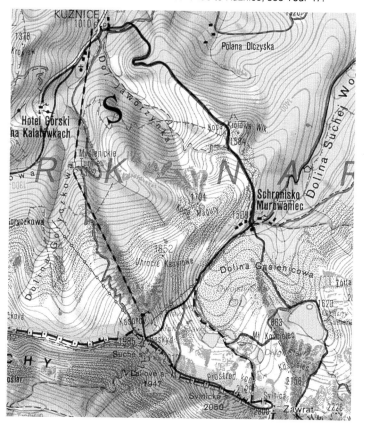

Index

The numbers behind the headwords relate to the page numbers.